Building Strong Churches

Dr. Michael Maiden

Unless otherwise indicated, all Scripture quotations are from The New King James Version (NKJV), copyright 1979, 1980, 1982, Thomas Nelson, Inc. Publishers. Used by permission. All rights reserved.

BUILDING STRONG CHURCHES
Copyright © 2017
by Dr. Michael Maiden

ISBN-13: 978-1979305198
ISBN-10: 1979305196

Published by
Joshua Generation Publishing
6225 N. Central Ave.
Phoenix, AZ 85012

Printed in the United States of America. All rights reserved under International Copyright Law. Contents and/or cover may not be reproduced in whole or part without the express written consent of the publisher.

CONTENTS

Introduction	i
Chapter One: The Ecclesia	1
Chapter Two: Vision	13
Chapter Three: Leadership	31
Chapter Four: Prayer	51
Chapter Five: Outreach	71
Chapter Six: Community	89
Chapter Seven: Communication	107
Chapter Eight: Worship	125

i

Introduction

Tired of hearing it said, "this is a must read for all"? This time it's true. Dr. Michael Maiden is no novice when it comes to knowing what principles are successful in building the Kingdom and what teaching is necessary in targeting the ecclesia. I have personally witnessed him establish and nurture a church to a growth of thousands in attendance every service. I also witnessed as he faced betrayal, lies and destruction of both the church and his hope (momentarily). Fixing his faith on the Word of God, rather than on man, he applied the principles he'd long taught and started over. Presently, he is shepherding a church with an international vision which is on the brink of spiritual explosion.

Not content to have only his own personal success, Pastor Maiden has written this, and other books, to help those who may be facing what he has come through in victory. He defines clear steps to follow in order for us to fulfill our calling. They are arrows with which we can hit the mark.

Iverna Tompkins
Phoenix, Arizona
2006

Chapter One:
The Ecclesia

The Lord Jesus Christ used these words to describe what He was going to build on the earth in Matt. 16: 18b: *"...upon this rock I will build My church and the gates of hell shall not prevail I against it."* The creator, founder and builder of the church is none other than Jesus Christ Himself. The church is His idea, His design, His desire. The church was created in heaven to be manifest on earth.

Ecclesia

In ancient Rome, the word "ecclesia" had its origin and usage in the time of the Caesars, the great rulers of the Roman Empire. k Rome expanded its governing territory through endless military conquests, it had then to establish its political-governmental rule in those newly conquered lands. In order to establish and maintain a successful rule in these distant and diverse lands, Rome developed a successful leadership-training method. In the first phase of the process, Rome chose and called into service local men and women who were perceived as potentially capable of fulfilling a leadership role for Rome in their homeland. These "called ones" (ecclesia) were then taken from their various cultures, languages and countries back to Rome. There they were brought into the presence of Rome's emperors - the Caesars. For the next few months, and even years, their very specific task was to study the mind, methods, attitudes and decision-making process of the Caesar. They were brought there to learn to think and take action like the emperor did.

Once Rome was confident that these "students" had successfully learned their lesson, they were then redeployed back into the many different regions of the world they had been gathered from. When they returned home, they were changed. Their home may have been in what we now call Spain, Germany or some other place, but now they no longer thought like the people in their region. Their minds had been filled with the laws and thoughts of Caesar. They brought the kingdom of Rome into these many lands by representing Caesar's mind and heart to the people they now ruled. This is what the church is to be in our world. It is where we sit at the feet of our Lord and learn His mind and heart so that we can then give an accurate representation of his Kingdom to the world we live in. The process begins when we come to the saving knowledge of Christ in New Birth and then participate in the life targeting the ecclesia of a Christ-honoring local church. That's the entry point to our personal "ecclesia." But there is no ending to the ongoing training and renewal that every believer in Christ Jesus is to experience. In their lifetime, no Christian is beyond the need for the church. No person is so mature and spiritually perfected that the many God-designed functions, blessing and graces the church produces are no longer necessary in their life. We will always need the church until Christ comes again or we call heaven our home.

Some will say that, because they've had a less-than-desirable experience with a church, they are then exempt from further participation in the church. As a minister, I freely acknowledge that in my own pastoral ministry and leadership, I have at times represented an imperfect and incomplete expression of the church. In comparison and contrast to the teaching and example the Word of God reveals to us about the power of the local church, we must admit to failing to meet many of the biblical expectations of the church. But our difficulties and even failures to build a church in harmony with the scriptures does not grant us immunity from our required membership in it. The church is God's ordained system and process for Christians to grow into maturity and then help others do likewise. Rather than pretend we can reject God's formula for spiritual life and maturity, let us all rededicate our lives to becoming the committed people that God can transform into His glorious church.

In this book, you will read what I've come to believe are targeting the ecclesia the ingredients that, when combined, make up the identity of a healthy, faithful and God-pleasing church. For thirty years I have served the church in full-time ministry. I grew up in a pastor's home and have ministered in churches allover the world. After studying many church models and what the Bible says about the church, I have written this book. My desire is to help pastors, leaders and all Christians become successful in building and participating in Christ-honoring and life-producing churches.

The Apostles Peter and John were on their way to afternoon prayer at the temple in Jerusalem. As they were about to enter into the Temple through the gate called Beautiful, a paralytic sitting outside the gate asked them for alms. Most probably these two had come and gone in and out of the temple through that same gate many times. Perhaps in those multitudes of prior visits they had passed by this very same man sitting at his post outside the gate. But that day was to be different. The Holy Spirit was about to bring a sudden and spectacular change into this suffering man's life. The scriptures record that, fastening his eyes on him, Peter looked down at this crippled man with Holy-Spirit-directed insight and intensity. He saw something about that man he hadn't seen before. He saw possibilities and potential that had never been realized. In fact, the Bible tells us that this man was born lame and had never taken a single step. He had to be carried by others to go anywhere. According to the Law of Moses, he was not permitted to go into the temple itself targeting the ecclesia because of his physical imperfection.

  The image of this man being right at the door but never entering into the temple becomes a metaphor for an innumerable multitude of men and women living in our world. They are close to, but just not quite in, the fullness of God's blessing and promise for their life. The name of the gate by which he sat was called Beautiful. The Greek translation of that name is horaios. Horaios comes from the Greek work hora which translates into English as "hour." Horaios literally means "the right hour or time; good timing; the right season." The season is called "beautiful" because when it's the right time and season it's always a beautiful thing. I believe that we have come into a season of "beautiful:" right and good timing as God's people. In this glorious season of visitation, all things are possible for those who believe.

As Peter looked at the man, the Holy Spirit awakened in Peter the sudden revelation that this man's Beautiful Time had now come, time for healing, restoration and destiny. Peter declared to the man, "In the Name of Jesus Christ of Nazareth, rise up and walk!" Then Peter reached out and took the man by the hand and lifted him up The man was gloriously healed that day at the gate called Beautiful. He was then miraculously able to do what he'd never done. The Bible declares he went walking and leaping and praising God.

I believe that right now God is releasing an anointing to heal the crippled walk of His children. He's going to enable you to do what you've never done before. Peter's command and outreached hand represent the apostolic authority of the five-fold ministry (apostles, prophets, evangelists, pastors and teachers) to bring healing and restoration to the body of Christ. We live in a time when God is restoring these essential offices and gifts to the church. Without apostles and prophets, the church remains crippled, unable to fulfill her destiny or reach her potential. How exciting it is to know that, just as the apostles raised up that man 2000 years ago, modern day apostles and prophets are unlocking a massive season of miraculous healing to the body of Christ.

The Bible then says that this formerly crippled man got up and entered into the temple. Through the authority of the kingdom of God represented in the ministry of the Apostle, the man now could go where he's never gone. He went into the temple. We are about to go into the temple of the last-day church.

The man couldn't enter the temple until he was healed. He couldn't be healed until he encountered apostolic power and authority. He couldn't encounter the Apostles until the right time had come.

Oh, but when there was a synergy of those ingredients, there then came an explosion of God's power and a transformation of a broken life. It's time. The right time has come for our lives to be connected to one another as living stones that together build the church. This is the hour for the healing and restoration of the church! This is the "beautiful" time when God has begun to restore the scriptural agencies (apostles and prophets) that have been given the spiritual authority to heal the crippled condition of the church. This is not the day to abandon and disengage from being a part of the church. We are in the beginning of a great season of visitation and grace that will leave us all transformed in incredible ways.

The promise of the hour is unique in all history. The Bible says the glory of the latter house shall be greater than the former (Hag. 2:9). Haggai's prophecy was never realized in the life of Israel, as its ultimate promise was for the church age. The last-day church is to receive a breadth and depth of God's magnificent glory that is incomparable to any other time in church history. We know and have studied the great testimonies of the early church through the record of the book of Acts and of the early writings of the church fathers.

Looking at the greatness of God's Spirit and grace that was lavished upon the early church, it would be easy to consign such a demonstration of power into a unique dispensation of time never to be repeated. But that's not the reality of God's promise for us. We live in the time of the greatest outpouring of God's Spirit that mankind has ever known! We also live in the time of "greater glory" of the church. As much as the early church experienced both quantitatively and qualitatively of God's power and promise, we are to experience more!

The first miracle of Jesus was at a wedding in Cana. He was there with His disciples and His mother. Often in that time and culture, wedding celebrations lasted for several days. For whatever reason (lack of adequate preparation, more guests than expected, more consumption than had been estimated) the host ran out of wine. Mary then asked, and even prodded, her son to solve that potentially embarrassing crisis for the host family. Jesus did so by filling empty vessels with water and then turning the water into wine. As the master of the feast tasted the miraculous supply of wine (not knowing where it had come from), he observed, "Most celebrations serve the good wine first and after it their cheaper, less valuable and tasty wine. But you have saved the best wine for last."

The church age will not come to an end with the church becoming tired, weak and frail, only a shadow of what it once was. The very opposite of that is true. The Lord saves the best for the last. In this, the final hour of the church, God is going to fulfill His promise and release to and through us the greatest move of His Spirit the world has ever known. No matter where we stand in relationship to the church Jesus promised to build, no matter how many disappointments, frustrations, failures and setbacks we've seen or experienced, no matter how painful our journey might have been so far, my precious friend, please know this truth: God is not done with the church. Our greatest hour is just beginning now!

Campus Martius

Jesus famously said in Matt. 22: 14, "*For many are called, but few are chosen.*" This was either a direct adaptation or an inferred understanding of the mission statement of the great Roman army.

Roman army

- No one was forced to serve in the army. Army service was the highest privilege of Roman citizenship.
- Military training began in early childhood.
- The Campus Martius was the great training ground in Rome where men were called from around the Roman Empire to learn and practice running, wrestling, fencing, javelin throwing, swimming, and so forth.
- All men between the ages of 17 and 45 were "called" to try out for military service.
- Only the best, strongest and most successful at the Campus Martius were chosen from the many participants by consuls. (The consuls would sit in grandstands or walk on the field while they studied those in training.)
- Officers were chosen and then appointed from those who had the best reputation at the Campus.
- Those called to the Campus Martius but then not chosen were not condemned but were graciously allowed to return to their occupations and families.
- Although all men were volunteered (called), only the best were chosen to serve.

The Church

The church is the "Campus Martius" for the Kingdom of God in the earth. We are all "called" through the saving grace of our loving God. As we arrive at the Campus to participate in a New-Testament church, we then begin our training regimen. As we receive teaching and training (discipleship), we grow stronger and more skilled at living an overcoming Christian life.

The church is the place where the greatness of men's and women's lives are discovered and developed. Being "chosen" has nothing to do with the whims or capriciousness of God (Of course, He has none.); instead, being "chosen" means having earned recognition for proven successes. The church is God's system and the process for renewing the minds and transforming the lives of His people. God has given specific, dynamic spiritual gifts to certain leaders for the development of the potential of His people. Just as the trained and experienced military instructors at Campus Martius worked closely with all the men who were called there, so God has specialized instructors in the church to accomplish for the His kingdom the same things the instructors did at Campus Martius.

Eph. 4:11-16 says, *He Himself gave some to be apostles, some prophets, some evangelists, and some pastors and teachers, for the equipping of the saints for the work of ministry, for the edifying of the body of Christ, til we all come to the unity of the faith and of the knowledge of the Son of God, to a perfect man, to the measure of the stature of the fullness of Christ; that we should no longer be children, tossed to and fro and carried about with every wind of doctrine, by the trickery of men, in the cunning craftiness of deceitful plotting, but, speaking the truth in love, may grow up in all things into Him who is the head - Christ - from whom the whole body, joined and knit together by what every joint supplies, according to the effective working by which every part does its share, causes growth of the body for the edifying of itself in love.*

Jesus gave certain gifts, commonly called "the five-fold ministry gifts," to men. These gifts are equipping anointings to heal and mature the body of Christ. It is through these five gifts that the person and power of Jesus Christ ministers to His people. The church cannot discover her greatest glory without the input and impartation of all five of these offices.

Although it is rare that all five are resident in a local body, they are available as traveling ministries to anyone who seeks them. We live in a time when, for the first time in centuries, God has graciously restored these gifts and anointings to the church. What this means is God's complete system for the perfecting (maturing) of the saints is now in the earth! The far reaching implication of the returning of these gifts has not yet been fully understood or realized by the church in general.

Read Eph. 4:8-16, except this time in the Message translation:

> *He climbed the high mountain, He captured the enemy and seized the booty, He handed it all out in gifts to the people. It's true, is it not, that the One who climbed up also climbed down, down to the valley of earth? And the One who climbed down is the One who climbed back up, up to highest heaven. He handed out gifts above and below,*

filled heaven with his gifts, filled earth with his gifts.

He handed out gifts of apostle, prophet, evangelist, and pastor-teacher to train Christians in skilled servant work, working within Christ's body, the church, until we're all moving rhythmically and easily with each other, efficient and graceful in response to God's Son, fully mature adults, fully developed within and without, fully alive like Christ.

No prolonged infancies among us, please. We'll not tolerate babes in the woods, small children who are an easy mark for impostors. God wants us to grow up, to know the whole truth and tell it in love-like Christ in everything. We take our lead from Christ, who is the source of everything we do. He keeps us in step with each other. His very breath and blood flow through us, nourishing us so that we will grow up healthy in God, robust in love.

The world has yet to see the fullness of what God will do in and through the church. We live in a time of transforming wineskins. The shape and structure of the church is being changed because *no one puts a piece of unshrunk cloth on an old garment; for the patch pulls away from the garment, and the tear is made worse. Nor do they put new wine into old wineskins, or else the wineskins break, the wine is spilled, and the wineskins are ruined. But they put new wine into new wineskins, and both are preserved.* (Matt. 9: 16-17)

The new wine of a heaven-sent glory tarries until the new wineskin of a scriptural church structure is formed. We will reach certain boundaries and restrictions that limit the expression of God's promised power and glory as long as our "wineskin" (church model) is in contrast to that of the scriptures. The scriptural pattern of how the church is to be configured unlocks the great promise and potential of all the church is promised to be, as Jesus declared in Matt. 16:18: *"I will build my church and the gates of hell shall not prevail against it."*

Chapter Two:
Vision

Vision comes first. Not only is it first in the sequence of the chapters of this book, but it must be the first priority in the building of a healthy, successful church. Everything else becomes entirely dependent and reliant on the clarity, strength and genuineness of the vision. The other principles in the following chapters are also tremendously necessary and important, but all of them are subject to the governing principle of Vision.

Vision is the nucleus, the center or gravity, around which all other principles revolve. It's not that vision alone is somehow more individually important than evangelism, prayer or discipleship, but that vision is the means by which these other valuable components find their definition and expression. Vision is the blueprint for the structure that the other tools and resources, working together, will successfully build. The blueprint comes before the building. The map comes before the journey. Vision comes first. *Where there is no vision, the people perish.* (Prov. 29:18, KJV)

A lack of vision is a recipe for failure. Looking at our church, we can many times misinterpret that which is visible and measurable, such as the numbers of people or the amount of energy, and activity, as indicators of success. But energy and activity without progress and achievement cannot be rightly declared as success. Without the principle and power of vision infusing direction, vitality, energy and unity into the life of a local church, that body will be incapable of fulfilling its calling or realizing its potential. The principle of vision applies to all of our lives as God's children and to the life of the church.

Vision is more than just a singular experience. It's a lifelong process and progression. Vision is something that expands, develops, increases and is clarified over time. Vision is a living principle that nourishes, encourages and motivates those who feed at her table regularly. God has created us to thrive under the presence and influence of vision in our lives. God has designed the church to thrive under the government of a God-breathed vision given to the pastor and embraced by the church.

Every life, church, business, city needs a vision in order to be successful. But we do not need just vision that we manufacture through our desires and imagination; one must have a God-given vision in order to be guaranteed a God-given success. God is the giver of vision. He gives vision to us so we can then take ownership of its great promise and experience its great reward. He goes to great lengths in order to be able to successfully communicate His predestined plan for our lives. Acts 2: 17 tells us:

> *"And it shall come to pass in the last days," says God, "That I will pour out of My Spirit on*

all flesh; Your sons and your daughters shall prophesy, Your young men shall see visions, Your old men shall dream dreams."

    Peter gave a scriptural explanation to thousands of curious spectators of what had happened in the outpouring of the Holy Spirit on the day of Pentecost. In the Apostle's message, there is the explanation not only of the events of that day, but also of the ongoing purpose of the Holy Spirit in the lives of God's people. With three different words the Bible gives us three different methods that essentially share one common goal and purpose. Visions, dreams and prophecy are the three words and methods that the Holy Spirit uses to accomplish one common purpose. That united purpose is to reveal God's will and purpose to our lives.
    The fact that this initial experience and the following explanation of the coming of the Holy Spirit to the church does not include any mention of speaking in tongues or of the other wondrous gifts the Holy Spirit empowers us to possess (1 Cor. 12) is important to note. In this "first mention" introduction of the Holy Spirit, we find a declaration of the essential role and function of the person and power of the Holy Spirit in the church. Visions, dreams, and prophecies are all methods of *communication*. The primary purpose and function of the Holy Spirit in relationship to God's people is the communication of God's will to them. That is what visions, dreams, and prophecies do - *communicate something*. God wants us to know about our Life and His will. At the very core of the strategic objective of the Holy Spirit Himself is a determination and spiritual empowerment to be a clear and successful channel of

communication from God to His people and to give us vision for our lives, churches, businesses, and so on.

These spiritual experiences (visions, dreams, prophecy) have a dynamically important design. They become spiritual interpretations for us to be able to understand the language of heaven on earth. God understands the importance of vision in the life of His people. He has gone to great lengths to supply our lives with the opportunity to secure a vision with the help of the Holy Spirit. After receiving a truly God-given dream, prophecy or vision, that spiritual experience is to then translate into an impartation or clarification of us having a vision for our lives.

The senior pastor at a local church has no greater role than being the visionary of that body of believers. No other activity, responsibility or duty carries more significance and importance than that of birthing, communicating and imprinting vision into the life of the congregation. No other person, internally in the structure of the church or externally through outside experts or opinion, has been empowered and authorized for this vital task.

A pastor who lacks vision for the church may be able to distract his and others attention from that failure through the business of the many other responsibilities and activities he or she has in their church role. The fact that a church continues to function and that the pastor may be greatly loved and appreciated by those he serves does not mean that all is well and something essential is not missing. It is. What a church can become, where it can go and what it can achieve are all expressed and achieved by a visionary who does what's necessary to obtain direction, purpose and meaning for his church through vision.

There is power in a God-given vision: power to release God's will to God's people, power to motivate, unite, excite, challenge, encourage and heal. Sometimes the seeming contrast of the simplicity of vision tempts us to undervalue and underestimate its tremendous importance. Nothing else must be allowed to overtake or eliminate the priority and position vision must have in relationship to the church.

What Is Vision?

Vision is not what we see with our physical eyes but what we perceive with our spiritual and mental sight. It is what we see about the future. Successful leaders have a vision for what they want to see happen in the future of their company, city, country or, in our case, church. Vision is a blueprint of something you want to build. It is a map of where you want to go.

It's not enough to have and communicate a vision. To be successful, a vision must be clearly articulated and understood. It must be the right vision for the right people and place and for the right time. For Christian leaders, a vision must be God-inspired, not just man-imagined. Only God is able to facilitate all that is required for a truly successful vision. He is the Father of dreams and visions and He longs to give birth to vision in our lives. He gives vision to those who seek Him.

Joseph had a dream (Gen. 37:5a). As a seventeen-year old youth, Joseph dreamed of greatness. Using two different metaphors, God imparted the same understanding to this young man: he was to rule, lead and be honored by his family.

His dreams became his vision. Something inside him bore witness to the promise his dreams declared to him. In spite of more than a decade of betrayal, imprisonment and loneliness, his vision remained strong. He lived with the aptitude and the attitude of a prince even when he was locked up in prison. The vision we have for the future determines how we live our lives today.

Our vision must have a spiritual origin. It must be more than the calculations of men's minds attempting to solve the problems in men's lives. It must be more than what we think we're capable of doing or achieving. It must be more than gathering the ideas and opinions borrowed from others and calling them our own. Joseph's dreams awakened a vision of destiny that from that point on passionately consumed his life. Real vision, given from God and birthed in our souls, unlocks real passion and purpose for our lives and churches.

There is no substitute or replacement for what vision is and what vision does in the life of a church. Great vision must not be complex, complicated or confusing. Great vision must be simple, comprehendible and inspired. God has a great vision for you and your church.

How Is Vision Discovered?

After Joseph successfully interpreted Pharaoh's dream, Pharaoh gave him the Egyptian name of Zaphnath Paaneah which means "God speaks and God lives." None of the Egyptian gods or their human servants could interpret Pharaoh's troubling dream. Only Joseph's God could, the one true living God that we love and serve. *Pharaoh said, "Your God speaks; therefore He surely lives."* His gods (the idols of Egypt) were dumb and deaf, wood and stone, mute and silent. But the God of Joseph had a voice.

How does vision come? It comes by our hearing what our God is speaking. Our God speaks and He lives! He speaks to us from His word, which lives and abides forever. He speaks to our inner man, with His still, small voice. He speaks to us through visions, dreams and prophecy. God is speaking but are we hearing and listening? Our difficulty is not with convincing God to talk to us; instead, it is with quieting our hearts in order to hear His voice.

Jesus saw what man could not see. One day He sent His disciples away to get some food. They weren't gone that long, but by the time they returned to Him, an entire city had been converted. They were in shock and disbelief. The people Jesus reached were considered unreachable. The way He reached them was unconventional. The disciples hadn't had a clue about what would happen that day. Jesus then taught them. In John 4:35 he said, *"Do you not say, 'There are still four months and then comes the harvest'? Behold, I say to you, lift up your eyes and look at the fields, for they are already white for harvest!"*

"There are yet four months and then comes the harvest" was a colloquial phrase in their culture about not worrying about today - tomorrow things will be better. Jesus was combating the error of that sentiment by introducing the power of vision to his disciples. He told them *to lift up their eyes*, not just their physical eyes but their spiritual eyes.

The *great harvest* Jesus reaped that day was the direct result of a *great vision*. He saw what His disciples did not and henceforth accomplished what they could not. Jesus was inviting them to the place of *harvest vision*. We as believers must join our Lord in the blessed place of seeing the fields white (ready) for harvest. The opportunity He seized was a reward of vision He had received. When we can see what others can't see, we can do what others can't do.

It came time for God to show Abraham his destiny, his inheritance and his future. *And the LORD said to Abram, after Lot had separated from him: "Lift your eyes now and look from the place where you are - northward, southward, eastward, and westward; for all the land which you see I give to you and your descendants forever."* (Gen. 13:14-15) The Lord told Abraham, "If you can see it, you can have it."

From the mountaintop, Abraham could see what he couldn't see from the plain. As we ascend God's mountain by seeking His face, we are positioned to receive insight that gives direction to our lives.

In ancient Greece there was a specific occupation that was called a *sophos*. A *sophos* was a watchman who would climb the mountains in order to see farther to the horizon and clearer in the heavens. He knew the movements of the heavenlies (stars) and was able then to navigate a successful course by interpreting the heavens. The Greek word for wisdom, *sophia*, comes from that word and concept. As we seek God for wisdom (direction, understanding, purpose, vision), we climb the mountain in our pursuit of His will. Then we have greater clarity and understanding in order to give direction to our lives.

Visionaries must be mountain-ascending watchmen who are willing to climb higher and see farther than others do. Descending the mountain, the watchman calms the fears and assuages the doubts of those at its bottom. He has been to the top and discovered vision there. He now knows where they are and where they're going.

Communicating the Vision

Hab. 2:1-3 reads:

> *I will stand my watch*
> *And set myself on the rampart,*
> *And watch to see what He will say to me,*
> *And what I will answer when I am corrected.*
> *Then the LORD answered me and said:*
> *"Write the vision*
> *And make it plain on tablets,*
> *That he may run who reads it.*
> *For the vision is yet for an appointed time;*
> *But at the end it will speak, and it will not lie.*
> *Though it tarries, wait for it;*
> *Because it will surely come,*
> *It will not tarry."*

People all around us are sitting, standing, stationary, unmoved and unmotivated, waiting for a man or woman of faith to bring God's vision and purpose into their lives. Anointed vision stirs and stimulates formerly passive and inactive people to begin to run into destiny. We are all made to run. It is *vision* that has the power to unlock our lives so we can experience the meaningful and satisfying life that God has created us for.

Write the Vision

Our vision must be clear, concise and readily understandable. If vision is of primary importance, then the quality of the communication of that vision holds sway over its success or failure. Communication is power. Good communication has the power to accomplish many tremendous things.

Very often the power of a vision loses its strength because of unsatisfactory communication. Communicate to others what you've heard and seen from God. Let that communication be written; let it be plain and clear so nothing is lost in its transmission from God to them. Once the vision has been successfully communicated to the church and the church has embraced and taken ownership of it, then there will be a willingness to wait for it, though it tarries.

Vision, Timelines and Goal Setting

At the end it will speak, and it will not lie. The vision that God imparts to pastors and churches has in it various timelines of fulfillment and completion. A God-imparted vision has in its DNA a God-appointed time of fulfillment. Some vision has a short timetable; other parts of vision have a longer timeline. Vision creates an expectation that generates the process of goal setting.

When Jesus fed the five thousand (that's men only, the crowd estimate is fifteen to twenty thousand people), He gave us an example of acquiring success through planning, preparation and strategy.

> *But He said to them, "How many loaves do you have? Go and see."*
> *And when they found out they said, "Five, and two fish."*
> *Then He commanded them to make them all sit down in groups on the green grass. So they sat down in ranks, in hundreds and in fifties. And when He*

had taken the five loaves and the two fish, He looked up to heaven, blessed and broke the loaves, and gave them to His disciples to set before them; and the two fish He divided among them all. So they all ate and were filled.

And they took up twelve baskets full of fragments and of the fish. Now those who had eaten the loaves were about five thousand men." (Mark 6:38-44)

Jesus saw what others could not see. He had a vision for feeding that great multitude. His vision then led to strategic planning and action.

First He required a complete inventory of all useful resources (in this case, any food). He instructed them to "Go and see" what they had to work with. When we discover what we have, we also become aware of what we don't have. This narrative is full of numbers. How many people needed to be fed? What resources did they have to work with? How many were there to serve the food? There were twelve disciples. How many baskets full of leftovers? There were twelve. The vision behind the miracle of feeding the multitude was entirely couched in an administrative structure that brought a seamless order to the event.

Secondly, Jesus divided the larger task of feeding 5000 (remember, that's just the men) into smaller, more manageable groups of fifties and hundreds. This example and its imagery is of a multitude being sectioned off into much smaller and much easier to serve ranks. That's what goal setting does for us. When the goals are reasonable, performable and obtainable, the larger vision can begin to be realized, as was the case here, one small group at a time. Though the conclusion of that day's event was truly, spectacularly supernatural, its fluid administration was anything but spectacular. From one small group to another, the disciples moved forward until all were fed. There was a beginning point, an in-between and eventually an ending. The process was so seamlessly managed that the disciples neglected to recognize how grandly supernatural it truly was.

Without strategic planning and goal setting, our vision cannot become a reality. God has a vision for every pastor and church. There is a strategic goal-setting wisdom for every vision. The same God who joyously and lovingly gives vision to pastors and churches will also give those pastors and churches the wisdom and goal-setting strategies that will enable them to succeed in their vision.

Refining the Vision

The vision of a church will eventually grow, evolve, refocus and refine itself. God adds to our vision, increasing its size and cope changing it primary focus. It's God s vision that we are sharing and stewarding. He can, and most of the time will, transform it a He chooses. In Mark 8:22-25, the Bible tell the tory of a blind man being healed by Jesus.

> *Then He came to Bethsaida; and they brought a blind man to Him, and begged Him to touch him. So He took the blind man by the hand and led him out of the town. And when He had spit on his eyes and put His hands on him,*

He asked him if he saw anything. And he looked up and said, "I see men like trees, walking."
   Then He put His hands on his eyes again and made him look up. And he was restored and saw everyone clearly.

   After Jesus initially prayed over this blind man, his vision was partially, imperfectly restored. When Jesus asked him what he saw, he said he saw objects and movement but lacked clarity and definition in his vision. Jesus didn't send him away with his vision only partially restored; He prayed over the man again until his vision was perfectly clear. Pastors and leaders who have need of the healing and refining of their vision need only to ask for it from the Lord. This second touch must be a regular and even frequent part of the development and growth of vision in our lives as pastors of churches.
   Many times God will change and redirect the focus of a pastor's and a church's vision. This redirection of vision requires flexibility and obedience on the behalf of God's people. Pastors and churches that refuse to heed the call for change in vision will suffer the consequence of lost momentum and diminished results as God's presence wanes from their midst.
   Having previous successes can become a hindrance to future success *if* leadership is incapable of facilitating vision redirection when God ordains it. Many formerly great churches, institutions and denominations are but a shadow of what they once were because of an inability to successfully adapt to a changing vision. The visionary and the vision that

once made them stay successful have been replaced by visionless caretakers of dying institutions.

Becoming the Vision

Moses wasn't just a delivery boy running errands for God. Moses didn't just deliver a message to Pharaoh; he became the message himself. Pastors are not assigned to be emotionally disengaged sermon givers and cold-hearted vision administrators.

The vision God gives a pastor for His church must become the passionate obsession of his entire life and ministry.

The pastor who has received the vision must also then become the vision himself. The attitude, action and agenda of the pastor must all be controlled and consumed by the vision his life's been assigned to express. If the pastor is passionless about the vision, why should the church care more than he does? If the vision seems unimportant to the pastor, why should it be of importance to the church members? Real vision produces real passion and real passion is contagious.

If a pastor lacks vision, he will ultimately lose his passion for ministry itself. If a pastor loses the passion for his vision, he must quickly reclaim it or seek the Lord for redirection or refinement concerning it. In some cases, a visionless pastor becomes an impediment to the well-being and growth of a church. If he is either incapable or unwilling to reclaim vision, he must, for the sake of the people, leave that church.

Conversely, if a pastor is convinced of a vision but feels his or her church is unwilling to embrace that vision, that pastor should leave that church. These will be, I hope, rare occasions in the lives of pastors and the church.

Pastors and Their Staffs

Vision must be constantly communicated. The pastoral staff and leadership of a local church must not only be knowledgeable of the church's vision, they must become passionate about it. For the leaders to share an excitement about the vision, they must be consistently reminded of the vision they're there to help facilitate. The pastor's responsibility is to nurture the vision of the house to those who labor in the house. As staff and leadership grow, there must be the indoctrination of the vision to those who are new to it. Pastors must understand the importance of being consistently repetitious in the communication of the vision of the church.

The pastoral staff and leadership of a church must also take ownership of the vision God has given the pastor for their church. There must be unity of hearts, minds, words and actions concerning the vision of the house. Once the staff takes ownership of the vision, they'll be able to refine and define it concerning their areas of leadership. It will become one vision with many different expressions in the life of the church.

The staff must take advantage of their influence with the church to confirm to the people the same vision the pastor shares with them. There must be an "echo" of the same purpose and vision from the staff and leaders as is heard from the senior pastor. Division, i.e., "two visions" ("di" = "two"), comes into a church because someone, usually another leader, has a different vision for the church than the pastor does. Common vision produces uncommon unity. When the leadership team of a church can overcome the obstacles and enemies of united vision, they will see their efforts greatly rewarded.

When the leadership of a church is negligent in consistently communicating the vision of the church to the people, there will always be remoteness and resistance in the life of those they're called to lead. While this attitude may be judged to be rebellion, it may actually only be uncertainty from those who have yet to be successfully exposed to the vision of the church. Leaders must remind themselves that many of those they minister to are unfamiliar with, and therefore uninfluenced, by the passions that drive the leaders.

Breaking through Limitations with Vision

The Hebrew word for "vision" is *chazon* which means "a prophetic vision, dream, oracle, revelation; to see, behold, perceive." In ancient Hebrew, the letters of the alphabet were originally word pictures, with each different letter representing a symbol. The letters in the ancient spelling of *chazon* means 'what you see when the fence is cut; seeing past the limitations and barriers." So vision is seeing past the walls and fences of our limitations and being given sight into what can be. The Holy Spirit is the instrument that "cuts through" our fences and gives us revelation of God's will and purpose.

Our actions, attitudes and words are dynamically influenced by our spiritual vision. In 2 Kings 6 there's a great story of me power of God-vision.

> *And when the servant of the man of God arose early and went out, there was an*

army, surrounding the city with horses and chariots. And his servant said to him, "Alas, my master! What shall we do?"

So he answered, "Do not fear, for those who are with us are more than those who are with them."

And Elisha prayed, and said, "LORD, I pray, open his eyes that he may see." Then the LORD opened the eyes of the young man, and he saw. And behold, the mountain was full of horses and chariots of fire all aroundElisha. (2 Kings 6:15-17)

Elisha and his young servant experienced identical life circumstances. The dichotomous reactions they had were based on each man's vision. The servant saw what his natural senses allowed him to see, the Syrian army ready to capture his master and him. He became fearful and confused not because of what he saw but because of what he didn't see. Elisha also saw the Syrian soldiers; he was fully aware of their presence.

But Elisha also saw the spiritual realities of that moment. His spiritual vision influenced and governed his natural vision and circumstances. He prayed and asked God to give his servant the same spiritual vision that he had.

Vision is everything. It is the difference between success or failure, victory or defeat, joy or sorrow, peace or fear, faith or confusion. We were not made to live visionless lives or pastor visionless churches or work in visionless jobs. The God who lovingly opened the eyes of Elisha's servant longs to open the eyes of His children today. *"Call to Me, and I will answer you, and show you great and mighty things, which you do not know."* (Jer. 33:3)

    If we call, He will answer. If we seek, we will find. If we hunger and thirst, we will be filled. Vision calls out to the church, to pastors and leaders, to men and women young and old. It awaits to be discovered and received. Vision is waiting in the presence of the Lord for those who've come seeking its treasure. There is no reason for us not to pursue what God has prepared for us.

Chapter Three:
Leadership

Vision is the blueprint of the house and leadership is its structure. No matter how magnificent the design may be, it cannot successfully become a reality without the structure of leadership in place. Leadership is the bone structure, the skeleton of the body itself.

The success of a vision will rise or fall according to the quality of the leadership stewarding it. There is no substitute for good leadership. The tremendous devastation that poor leadership, or none at all, produces is apparent everywhere you look. Much of the pain and suffering mankind experiences and endures is a direct result of someone in leadership failing their responsibility. All of us have experienced the influence of both good and poor leadership. All of us have also at one time or another been successful or unsuccessful in various leadership roles. Leadership matters.

The Fall of Man

The original sin was the result of failed leadership. There is no doubt that when God created man He gave him authority and responsibility to accomplish His will on earth. This was a leadership mandate and expectation as clearly stated in Gen. 1:8: *Then God blessed them, and God said to them, "Be fruitful and multiply; fill the earth and subdue it; have dominion over the fish of the sea, over the birds of the air, and over every living thing that moves on the earth."*

By this tremendous mandate, God was giving man the primary leadership and stewardship of the earth. God had put Adam and Eve in charge. What went wrong? Eve was beguiled by a serpent she was empowered to rule over. Adam abdicated his responsibilities entirely. He apparently was not even the leader in the home and hadn't trained his wife in the knowledge of God's will. Then when his wife was deceived into sin, instead of driving the serpent and his lies from his family, he consequently joined in her sin without even putting up a fight:

> Now the serpent was more cunning than any beast of the field which the Lord God had made. And he said to the woman, "Has God indeed said, 'You shall not eat of every tree of the garden'?"
> And the woman said to the serpent, "We may eat the fruit of the trees of the garden; but of the fruit of the tree which is in the midst of the garden, God has said, 'You shall not eat it, nor shall you touch it, lest you die.'"

Then the serpent said to the woman, "You will not surely die. For God knows that in the day you eat of it your eyes will be opened, and you will be like God, knowing good and evil."

So when the woman saw that the tree was good for food, that it was pleasant to the eyes, and a tree desirable to make one wise, she took of its fruit and ate. She also gave to her husband with her, and he ate. Then the eyes of both of them were opened, and they knew that they were naked; and they sewed fig leaves together and made themselves coverings.

And they heard the sound of the Lord God walking in the garden in the cool of the day, and Adam and his wife hid themselves from the presence of the Lord God among the trees of the garden.

Then the Lord God called to Adam and said to him, "Where are you?"

So he said, "I heard Your voice in the garden, and I was afraid because I was naked; and I hid myself."

And He said, "Who told you that you were naked? Have you eaten from the tree of which I commanded you that you should not eat?" (Gen. 3:1-11)

God gave us the power of choice. He gave his children the option of choosing or rejecting him and his will. He needs to be chosen. Successful leadership is revealed by those who make right choices. We fight the same human vulnerabilities that Adam did:

- Hidden suspicions of the real intentions of God for our lives.
- Satan's assault on the truthfulness of God's word
- Weakness to the presence of temptation (Every successful leader recognizes his personal weaknesses and seeks grace to overcome them while being diligent to resist temptation in those areas.)
- Hiding our failures from God
- Covering them with inadequate means and devices
- Abandoning our leadership post when others need us the most.
- Making bad decisions because of fear
- Feeling "naked" (Sin consciousness produces an army of negative conditions: failure, fearfulness, rejection, shame, self-hatred, depression, hopelessness and so forth.)
- A disposition to question, resist and rebel against authority.
- Refusal of personal accountability (blame shifting)

Let us be extremely thankful that, as massive and pervasive as Adam's transgression was, God had a solution. That wondrous answer is the glorious Jesus Christ. He did what Adam would not. His example and leadership were perfect in every way.

Whenever leadership is absent, has failed or has been rejected, there will always be negative consequences. Look at what happened to godly leadership in Judg. 21:25: *In those days there was no king in Israel; everyone did what was right in his own eyes.* Moral relativism was the unfortunate result of the absence of leadership. Without proper leadership, people just made up their own rules. With no obvious standard to follow, people created their own standards then lived their lives accordingly. The absence of leadership created a vacuum filled by immorality and godlessness.

Leadership Is God's Answer

No matter what the problem or circumstance, God's answer will always be the same: leadership! The first thing God does in response to man's need is to raise up leaders. *"So I sought for a man among them who would make a wall, and stand in the gap before Me on behalf of the land, that I should not destroy it; but I found no one."* (Eze. 22:30)

Leadership is a calling and anyone can answer the call. The cry of Jesus was for God to raise up leaders. Jesus ministered to multitudes but mentored only twelve men to be leaders.

> *Then Jesus went about all the cities and villages, teaching in their synagogues, preaching the gospel of the kingdom, and healing every sickness and every disease among the people. But when He saw the multitudes, He was moved with compassion for them, because they were weary and scattered, like sheep having no shepherd. Then He said to His disciples, "The harvest truly is plentiful, but the laborers are few. Therefore pray*

> the Lord of the harvest to send out laborers into His harvest."
> And when He had called His twelve disciples to Him, He gave them power over unclean spirits, to cast them out, and to heal all kinds of sickness and all kinds of disease. Now the names of the twelve apostles are these: first, Simon, who is called Peter, and Andrew his brother; James the son of Zebedee, and John his brother; Philip and Bartholomew; Thomas and Matthew the tax collector; James the son of Alphaeus, and Lebbaeus, whose surname was Thaddaeus; Simon the Cananite, and Judas Iscariot, who also betrayed Him. (Matt. 9:35-38; 10:1-4)

The laborers are leaders; leadership is a labor. Jesus had, and still has, a great vision of the harvest. His answer then and now is to raise up leaders.

Understanding Kingdom Authority

Leadership is an expression of authority. No matter how great or small the task, successful leadership receives and releases authority to fulfill the responsibility. God does not invite us to accept the place of leadership without also imparting the necessary authority to accomplish the mission. In this New Testament passage, a great insight into kingdom authority is revealed:

> Now when Jesus had entered Capernaum, a centurion came to Him, pleading with Him, saying, "Lord, my

servant is lying at home paralyzed, dreadfully tormented."

And Jesus said to him, "I will come and heal him." The centurion answered and said, "Lord, I am not worthy that You should come under my roof. But only speak a word, and my servant will be healed. For I also am a man under authority, having soldiers under me. And I say to this one, 'Go,' and he goes; and to another, 'Come,' and he comes; and to my servant, 'Do this,' and he does it."

When Jesus heard it, He marveled, and said to those who followed, "Assuredly, I say to you, I have not found such great faith, not even in Israel! And I say to you that many will come from east and west, and sit down with Abraham, Isaac, and Jacob in the kingdom of heaven. But the sons of the kingdom will be cast out into outer darkness. There will be weeping and gnashing of teeth."

Then Jesus said to the centurion, "Go your way; and as you have believed, so let it be done for you." And his servant was healed that same hour. (Matt. 8:5-13)

The man in this narrative was a soldier, a centurion, meaning he led a company of one hundred men. What he said to Christ revealed his insight into how kingdom authority
works.

- To have authority, you must first be under authority.
- To the degree that you submit to authority, you will express it.
- To be a successful leader, you must first be a successful follower.
- Good followers make good leaders. Bad followers make bad leaders; great followers make great leaders.
- Both following and leading are acts of faith.

As pastors we must never commit authority or responsibility to those who won't submit. In writing to Timothy, Paul said that Timothy was to commit these to faithful men who will be able to teach others also. (2 Tim. 2:2) We are tempted as leaders to look for gifted men and then hope they become faithful. But God said to find faithful men and women and trust God to expand their giftedness.

The Four Laws of Leadership

Inclusive to all kingdom leaders are four dynamics: modeling, mentoring, motivation and multiplying.

1.) Modeling

The greatest, most effective and most spiritually dynamic law of leadership is found in modeling. Gideon was about to lead a small company of 300 men against a massive army of 100,000. Gideon's men had been handpicked from his army of 32,000 as the best candidates for their incredible assignment.

Now these men had been chosen for a task that must have been daunting to them. As they wrestled with their own fears and uncertainty, they were in desperate need of godly leadership. Gideon knew what God had called him to do. He had had a powerfully personal experience with the Lord in preparation for this great assignment. He also must have known what his men were struggling with and he had the solution. He would model for them what they would then do.

> *Then he divided the three hundred men into three companies, and he put a trumpet into every man's hand, with empty pitchers, and torches inside the pitchers.*
> *And he said to them, "Look at me and do likewise; watch, and when I come to the edge of the camp you shall do as I do: When I blow the trumpet, I and all who are with me, then you also blow the trumpets on every side of the whole camp, and say, 'The sword of the Lord and of Gideon!'"*
> *So Gideon and the hundred men who were with him came to the outpost of the camp at the beginning of the middle watch, just as they had posted the watch; and they blew the trumpets and broke the pitchers that were in their hands. Then the three companies blew the trumpets and broke the pitchers- they held the torches in their left hands and the trumpets in their right hands for blowing- and they cried, "The sword of the Lord and of Gideon!"* (Judg. 7: 16-20)

Gideon modeled three phases of leadership for his men, that we as leaders need to incorporate into our lives: blowing trumpets, breaking pitchers, and shouting.

Blowing Trumpets
When a group of leaders all say the same thing, there is a powerful result. As we speak God's word and raise up others to speak the same word, it becomes a powerful tool in reaching cities, setting people free and building churches. The trumpet itself is a metaphor for "prophetic truth," that which God is saying now to his people. Leadership means hearing and then speaking. We hear God's voice (trumpet) and then declare it to others, who then declare it themselves, and so on.

Breaking Pitchers
The next phase of modeling leadership is more difficult than the first. We tend to love pronouncing the word and wi!' of God to others. It's like blowing Gideon's trumpet. But it's an entirely different matter when the Lord asks us to break our pitchers.

In our present culture, leaders are taught and trained to hide any and all weaknesses from those they lead. But in the kingdom of God, godly leadership by modeling requires genuine brokenness in the life of the leader.

When Gideon broke his pitcher, the men then followed and broke their own pitchers. Our Gideon, Jesus Christ, has given us the supremely perfect example of the power of brokenness. He opened his life for all to see. And once he did that, something powerful took place.

Inside of the empty pitchers were lit torches. The light of the torch could not be seen until the pitcher was broken. When the vessels broke, the light could then shine. The lights represent the hidden glory in the heart of men. It can only be released through genuine brokenness before God and man.

We see the same principle in action in the life of Jesus as well. When Jesus appeared to his disciples after the resurrection, He initially had tremendous difficulty in gaining their attention and trust. But that soon changed.

> *On the evening of that first day of the week, when the disciples were together, with the doors locked for fear of the Jews, Jesus came and stood among them and said, "Peace be with you!"*
> *After he said this, he showed them his hands and side. The disciples were overjoyed when they saw the Lord. Again Jesus said, "Peace be with you! As the Father has sent me, I am sending you."* (John 20:19-21)

The sermon Jesus preached ("Peace be with you!") couldn't register in the hearts and minds of the disciples until they saw his scars. It wasn't until after they had touched his scars that they heard His message.

Trumpets without broken pitchers will never win the day and change people's lives. But if we blow the trumpet of truth and break the vessel of our lives, victory will come.

The Shout

The last modeling action Gideon took was to lead his men in a great shout: "The sword of the Lord and of Gideon!" The reality is that God has chosen to partner with us for the interest and advancement of His kingdom. What an unbelievable privilege: to work for and with God for the accomplishment of His will in the earth! As many have said, "We cannot without God; God will not without us."

Within Gideon's shout, there is something very significant that we need to catch hold of: when Gideon said "the sword of the Lord and of Gideon," he wasn't just making a nice little declaration. He was proclaiming the word of the Lord. The writer of Hebrews calls the word the "two-edged sword." The Greek word for "two-edged sword" is *distomos*. It is a composite of two words: *di* meaning "two" and *stomos* meaning "mouth." *Distomos* literally means "the two-mouthed sword."

So when Gideon was shouting the word of the Lord, he was declaring what he had heard and adding his mouth to it. As leaders, we hear what comes from God's mouth to our heart and then we declare what we have heard. When we say what God has said, both sides of the sword are formed and it becomes a great weapon of kingdom victory. Leaders have the obligation to hear and speak God's will.

"Look at me and do what I do!" Gideon didn't ask his men to do anything he wasn't willing to do himself first. He led by example. Real leadership is not asking others to do what we're not willing to do. Leaders must go where they are asking others to go.

In the New Testament, all that Jesus Christ did was show us a modeling form of leadership. The Apostle Peter was a product of His modeling. And Peter took that truth and passed it on to the church. Writing to the church in 1 Peter, he said, *The elders who are among you I exhort, who am also an elder and a witness of the sufferings of Christ, and also a partaker of the glory that shall be revealed: feed the flock of God which is among you, taking the oversight of them, not by constraint but willingly, not for filthy lucre but out of a ready mind, neither as being lords over God's heritage, but by being examples to the flock And when the Chief Shepherd shall appear, ye shall receive a crown of glory that fadeth not away.* (1 Pet. 5: 1-4)

The Greek word for "examples" is *tupos,* which means "a model for imitation, pattern, print, a stamp or scar, a shape, a statue." It also means "a prototype of that which was yet to be developed."

Tupos comes from the roots word *tupto* which means "to thump, cudgel or pummel; to strike with repeated blows with an instrument or hammer." Being an example (tupos) means we have surrendered to the process (tupto, "to strike with repeated blows"). The picture is of an artist carving a work out of stone. He is able to picture in his mind what he can make the undeveloped stone to look like. By chiseling the stone, the sculptor begins to change its form and appearance. With very blow, progress is gradually made until the artist is satisfied with his completed work.

Leaders are to be patterns and models on display for replication. Jesus led by this powerful principle. He invited his disciples to *"follow Me."* (Matt. 4: 19; 8:22, 16:24)

The Apostle Paul used the am principle in his leadership style. *Be ye followers of me, even as I also am of Christ.* (1 Cor. 11:1, KJV)

Being a leader is to submit to the molding work of the word of God and the Holy Spirit. Our God knows how to shape our lives into the image of Christ if we will just stay committed to the process that is bringing transformation into our lives. Modeling is the most successful leadership principle there will ever be.

2.) Mentoring

Successful leadership is balanced between the twin dynamics of teaching and training. Teaching is a vital component in the development of mature Christians but so is training. When one is absent or less than the other, the results we desire will be incomplete. The church, as with many educational and leadership models, has a tendency to be overbalanced on the teaching side of the equation. Without diminishing the importance of teaching, we know that information without application doesn't bring about results in people's lives.

When my three older children were old enough to drive a car, my job was to teach and train them how to drive. There is only so much you can "teach" about driving until you must "train" by allowing them to sit in the driver's seat and drive the car.

Joshua displayed this principle when he mentored the young princes of Israel:

> *And it came to pass, when they brought out those kings unto Joshua, that Joshua called for all the men of Israel, and said unto the captains of the men of war who went with him, "Come near, put your feet upon the necks of these kings." And they came near and put their feet upon the necks of them.*
>
> *And Joshua said unto them, "Fear not, nor be dismayed. Be strong*

and of good courage, for thus shall the Lord do to all your enemies against whom ye fight."
(Josh. 10:24-25)

    That day's victory for Israel was more than just a successful strategy that led to a victorious outcome. Joshua was mentoring the leaders of Israel. The five kings that Israel faced had hid themselves in a cave. At that time in history, people had come to believe the myth that kings were deities. They were afraid of them and attributed supernatural powers to their lives.

    Joshua knew these five kings were just men and that God had empowered Israel to conquer them. His goal that day was to teach and train the leaders of Israel in the knowledge of that same truth: they had authority over all the inhabitants of Canaan, including the kings.

    One by one Joshua called the men of Israel to come and put their feet on the necks of the kings. These men may have believed that Joshua could do that because of his place of exalted leadership in Israel. That day they learned that they could do it too. This "hands-on" training was a transforming life lesson that changed their beliefs, expectations and self image. They did what they didn't know they were capable of because Joshua had successfully mentored them.

    What would have happened *if* it had been only Joshua who put his feet on the kings' necks? The same victory would have been won, but the resulting consequences would have been radically different. The men of Israel would have looked to Joshua to do for them what they were unsure they themselves could do. It is a temptation in existing leadership to always be a "doer" because "doing" allows us to be honored and needed by others. Mentoring helps others become "doers" and therefore expands the scope of Christian ministry.

Jesus mentored his disciples. He taught and trained them and then sent them out to do the work. He successfully "coached" them as they entered into the ministry. The "fathering" and "mother" of leaders is essential to the making of "sons" and "daughters." *Behold, I will send you Elijah the prophet before the com ing of the great and dreadful day of the Lord. And he will turn the hearts of the fathers to the children, and the hearts of the children to their fathers, lest I come and strike the earth with a curse.* (Mal. 4:5-6)

The absence of role models, mentors, life coaches and natural and spiritual fathers creates a crisis. Incredible damage is done ("a curse") when children, natural or spiritual, are fatherless. The answer is found by raising up "a fathering spirit" in the home and church. God also places a "sonship" heart in His people who desire and are willing to be mentored.

3.) Motivating
One of the most important functions of any level of leadership is to motivate and encourage those you lead. Inspired lives inspire lives. Most leaders are, at some personal level, self-motivated men and women. They are people that have learned to feed their minds and hearts the healthy ingredients of various resources that ignite inspiration and motivation.

Leaders are aware of the influence their attitudes, words and actions have on those they're called to lead. We've all had the demoralizing experience of dealing with a discouraging, negative leader in our life. To truly inspire and motivate others, we must ourselves be inspired and motivated. Leaders must diligently protect and preserve their own emotional and life health.

King David endured the loss of all his material possessions, the kidnapping of his family and the utter destruction of his home and city. His men endured the same traumatic losses and sat down and wept until there were no more tears to cry. While his men progressed from sorrow to anger, David's response to the same tragedy was very different. It is a life lesson for us on emotional healing and health. *Now David was greatly distressed, for the people spoke of stoning him, because the soul of all the people was grieved, every man for his sons and his daughters. But David strengthened himself in the Lord his God.* (1 Sam. 30:6)

David accepted responsibility for his emotional condition and did something positive about it: he turned to God for help. David fought several battles that day and soon thereafter, as well, but none were as consequential as the battle he waged to reclaim his emotional health. He so conquered his own emotional turmoil that he shortly was able to motivate his discouraged men. They ended up retrieving everything that had been stolen, plus more, all because David, their targeting the ecclesia leader, encouraged and motivated himself.

In the New Testament book of Acts, the principle of motivation is clearly seen in a man named Joseph. *And Joseph, who was also named Barnabas by the apostles (which is translated Son of Encouragement), a Levite of the country of Cyprus...* (Acts 4:36) Because the disciples recognized the tremendous gift Joseph had to motivate and encourage others, they surnamed him Barnabas, "son of encouragement." Barnabas exemplified the spirit of encouragement in the life of a godly leader.

- He believed in Paul while the Apostles were still fearful and uncertain. (Acts 9:27)
- He encouraged the church at Antioch to continue with the Lord with purpose of heart. (Acts 11:23)
- He persuaded them to continue in the faith. (Acts 13:43)
- He strengthened the souls of the disciples, exhorting them to continue in the faith. (Acts 14:22)
- He refused to give up and abandon John Mark in spite of Paul's insistence that John Mark not be brought on a missionary journey (Acts 15:37-39), and later, Paul acknowledged that he was wrong in giving up on young John Mark (2 Tim. 4:21)

The word for "encouragement" comes from the Greek word *parakletos,* a word used for Christ and the Holy Spirit he sent to us. *Parakletos* has five synonymous meanings: "comforter, counselor, teacher, intercessor and helper." The Holy Spirit Himself brings all these attributes and anointings into our lives. Men and women who are filled with the Holy Spirit, like Barnabas, will also display the same attributes. Barnabas was an encourager and a motivator. In every contact that people had with him, he left them better off than they were before he came into their lives. May God help us as leaders to use every contact with those we lead, to leave them better off: strengthened, encouraged, inspired and motivated.

4.) Multiplying
Multiplication is the goal of the other laws of leadership. We model, mentor and motivate so that ultimately we can multiply. All that Jesus Christ did in modeling, mentoring, and motivating culminated in the multiplication of his life into twelve other men. Those men were an extension and expansion of all that Christ was. They changed the world in their lifetimes. And when He left, His influence not only stayed, it increased through these men.

Success without a successor is failure. Leaders must develop more leaders. There is tremendous strategic value in leaders' reproducing themselves. The goal of a leader should be to work himself out of a job by developing others to do the work.

GLOSSARY OF NEW TESTAMENT LEADERSHIP

TITLE	ROLE
APOSTLE	Births local churches, establishes and oversees ministries, ministers the word, is a spiritual father (Eph. 4: 11; 1 Cor. 12:28; Acts 2:43)
PROPHET	Reveals God's word, will and the future; releases destiny, calling, and Anointing of God's people (Eph. 4: 11, 2:20; Acts 11:27-30,13:1-4)

TITLE	ROLE
EVANGELIST	Wins souls and equips Christians to be soul-winners, helps start churches with teams (Eph. 4: 11, 2 Tim. 4:5, Acts 21:8)
PASTOR	Oversees, feeds, leads and cares for local church (Eph. 4:11; 1 Pet. 5:1-3)
TEACHER	Teaches correct doctrine and principles of the kingdom of God (1 Cor. 12:28, 2 Tim. 2:2,24)
ELDER	Leads and shepherds the church, a mature leader trusted with authority (I Tim. 4:14, 5:17-19)
BISHOP	Oversees, protects and helps church (1 Tim. 3: 1-8, Titus 1: 7, 1 Pet. 2:25)
DEACON	Handles business and practical needs of the church (Acts 6: 1-6, 1 Tim. 3:8, 12)

Chapter Four:
Prayer

Vision is the blueprint and leadership is the structure but prayer is the firm foundation upon which all else rests. The strength of the foundation determines the height and weight of the entire structure. Great vision and leadership require great prayer for great results.

    The importance and priority of prayer in a local church must be on the same footing as vision, leadership, evangelism or any other endeavor. Prayer must be made to be seen as vitally important and irreplaceable in the life of a local church. Prayer produces the very power of God that we must have to reach our cities, win the lost and build strong churches. A powerful church will be a praying church. A prayerless church cannot be a powerful one in the true supernatural graces of God. Without a successful prayer strategy and its implementation in our church, we doom our ministry efforts to mediocrity at best.

    Jesus visited the temple in Jerusalem just after His triumphant entry into Jerusalem. He found it out of order and He became angry at the activities and agendas that were present.

> *Then Jesus went into the temple of God and drove out all those who bought and sold in the temple, and overturned the tables of the money changers and the seats of those who sold doves. And He said to them, "It is written, 'My house shall be called a house of prayer,' but you have made it a den of thieves."*
>
> *Then the blind and the lame came to Him in the temple, and He healed them. But when the chief priests and scribes saw the wonderful things that He did, and the children crying out in the temple and saying, "Hosanna to the Son of David!" they were indignant and said to Him, "Do You hear what these are saying?"*
>
> *And Jesus said to them, "Yes. Have you never read, 'Out of the mouth of babes and nursing infants You have perfected praise'?"* (Matt. 21: 12-16)

These four results followed Christ's visit: purification, prayer, power and praise.

1.) Purification

Jesus drove out inappropriate behavior and attitudes from the temple. The same kind of attitudes and action com as a substitute for real prayer. The temple was being abused through these activities that were not a part of its d sign and purpose. Whenever any activity becomes a replacement for God's purpose, that activity must be changed and our lives and church purified so we can reclaim God's created design and purpose. What we do instead of prayer may not be seen as "evil" itself, but if we allow it to usurp the place of prayer, then becomes a problem.

Purification is a renewing and a realigning with godly priorities and purpose. Because it is easy for any of us as individuals to fall into the traps of misplaced priorities, it is, of course, easy for churches to do the same. Jesus drove out the problem and brought a restored purity to the temple.

2.) Prayer

Jesus gave us God's vision, the mission statement of what the church is called to be: "a house of prayer." When Mary and I have guests come to our house, they come to "the Maiden house." It's our house because we live there. The church is called "a house of prayer" because prayer lives there. Prayer owns, occupies and governs the house. We are called as pastors, leaders and church members to reclaim God's original desire and calling for the church to be a house of prayer.

A great prayer revival is beginning allover the world. God is calling His people back to the place of his presence and power, the place of prayer. *If My people who are called by My name will humble themselves, and pray and seek My face, and turn from their wicked ways, then I will hear from heaven, and will forgive their sin and heal their land.* (2 Chron.7:14) Prayer can change a city, a state, a nation. Our *land* can be healed if God's people humble themselves and pray. Could this be the reason for the great resistance that seems to arise whenever a church decides to become a house of prayer? Satan does not want our land healed. He knows if he can successfully distract and detour us from prayer, he can maintain his oppressive hold over the nations.

The early church prayed continuously, fervently and scripturally.

And they continued steadfastly in the apostles' doctrine and fellowship, in the breaking of bread, and in prayers. (Acts 2:42)

Now Peter and John went up together to the temple at the hour of prayer, the ninth hour. (Acts 3: 1)

So when they heard that, they raised their voice to God with one accord and said: "Lord, You are God, who made heaven and earth and the sea, and all that is in them, who by the mouth of Your servant David have said: 'Why did the nations rage, And the people plot vain things? The kings of the earth took their stand, And the rulers were gathered together Against the Lord and against His Christ.'
"For truly against Your holy servant Jesus, whom You anointed, both Herod and Pontius Pilate, with the Gentiles and the people of Israel, were gathered together to do whatever Your hand and Your purpose determined before to be done. Now, Lord, look on their threats, and grant to Your servants that with all boldness they may speak Your word, by stretching out Your hand to heal, and that signs and wonders may be done through the

name of Your holy servant Jesus." (Acts 4:24-30)

And when they had prayed, the place where they were assembled together was shaken; and they were all filled with the Holy Spirit, and they spoke the word of God with boldness. Now the multitude of those who believed were of one heart and one soul; neither did anyone say that any of the things he possessed was his own, but they had all things in common.
    And with great power the apostles gave witness to the resurrection of the Lord Jesus. And great grace was upon them all. Nor was there anyone among them who lacked; for all who were possessors of lands or houses sold them, and brought the proceeds of the things that were sold... (Acts 4:31-34)

Seven things happened as a result of their fervent prayer as seen in Acts 4:31-34:
    1. The place was shaken.
    2. They were all filled with the Holy Spirit.
    3. They spoke the word of God with boldness.
    4. They were of one heart and one mine (unity).
    5. The apostles gave powerful witness.
    6. Great grace washed upon them all.
    7. None of them lacked.

...but we will give ourselves continually to prayer and to the ministry of the word. (Acts 6:4)

And when he observed him, he was afraid, and said, "What is it, lord?" So he said to him, "Your prayers and your alms have come up for a memorial before God..." (Acts 10:4)

Peter was therefore kept in prison, but constant prayer was offered to God for him by the church. (Act 12:5)

And when they had fasted and prayed, and laid their hands on them, they sent them away. (Acts 13:3)

But at midnight Paul and Silas were praying and singing hymns to God, and the prisoners were listening to them. Suddenly there was a great earthquake, so that the foundations of the prison were shaken; and immediately all the doors were opened and everyone's chains were loosed. (Acts 16:25-26)

And it happened that the father of Publius lay sick of a fever and dysentery. Paul went in to him and prayed, and he laid his hands on him and healed him. (Acts 28:8)

Prayer was at the very center of the belief and behavior of the early church. With every mention of its practice there is also a recording of its results. Good things happen when God's people pray.

3.) Power
Then the blind and the lame came to them in the temple and they healed them. The temple was purified by the passion of Christ in order to reestablish its God-ordained purpose to be a house of prayer. Immediately after this transformation occurred, miracles began to take place. Prayer produces power. God's power began to flow when God's people began to pray. The "power shortage" that exists in much of the church today is a result of prayerlessness.

When the early church prayed in Acts 4, they were filled with supernatural boldness, supernatural power, supernatural grace and unity. Power began to manifest as soon as the church began to pray. The quality and fruitfulness of our Christian life is directly related to the quality and faithfulness of our prayer life. The scriptures say in 1 Tim. 2: 1: *Therefore I exhort first of all that supplications, prayers, intercessions, and giving of thanks be made for all men.*

Prayer must precede effort and action in the church. It must be our first priority and practice. The power we need to be the people we're called to be and to do things we're called to do is readily available for all of us in God's presence through prayer. The church, absent the power of God, becomes incapable of fulfilling her apostolic mission and ministry.

Because we must have God's power in order to succeed, we must bathe our lives and churches in unceasing prayer. *As* Paul said, *"Pray without ceasing."* (I Thess. 5: 17) Don't shut the power supply off, but keep the power flowing by uninterrupted prayerfulness.

4.) Praise

Of course your church praises and worships, so does mine. But I'm struck by the pronouncement of not just praise but "perfected praise." Praise that has realized its maturity and fulfilled its potential. Praise that follows after purity, prayer and power.

Those who personally witnessed the operation of the power of God began to passionately worship the person of God. This quality of praise required no training seminars or in-depth instruction. Instead it was the automatic response of the human soul and spirit to the demonstration of God's power, the power that was released when prayer was restored.

There is a previously unknown depth of passion, intensity and intimacy that erupts from a people personally witnessing and genuinely experiencing God's presence and power. "Perfect praise" is the result of encountering God's power. God's power is the result of prayer. Praying churches will discover a maturing and perfecting of their praise. Praise responds in gratitude to God for what prayer has released to men. *But You are holy, enthroned in the praises of Israel.* (Ps.22:3) *But thou art holy, o thou that inhabits the praises of Israel.* (Ps. 22:3)

The Hebrew word for "praise" here is *tehilla*, "spontaneous songs of worship; spiritual songs." God enthrones Himself in praise that is completely genuine in its expression as a spontaneous act of adoration. That kind of praise arises in the hearts of a people that have freshly experienced God's grace and glory. The newness of that experience produces the "new song" of the heart. A praying people will always be a praising people. As they continue to have new experience with God, they joyously answer back with new expressions of praise and worship. *"Ask, and you will receive, that your joy may be full."* (John 16:24b) Pray for and then *receive* God's *promises* and your praise will be perfected your joy *will* be *full.*

Praying Churches Have Praying Pastors

Jesus lived His life as a man of constant prayer. He has not asked us to be or do anything that He first has not been or done.

> *Now in the morning, having risen a long while before daylight, He went out and departed to a solitary place; and there He prayed.* (Mark 1:35)

> *And when He had sent them away, He departed to the mountain to pray.* (Mark 6:46)

> *So He Himself often withdrew into the wilderness and prayed.* (Luke 5:16)

> *Now it came to pass in those days that He went out to the mountain to pray, and continued all night in prayer to God.* (Luke 6:12)

> *Now it came to pass, about eight days after these sayings, that He took Peter, John, and James and went up on the mountain to pray. As He prayed, the appearance of His face was altered,*

and His robe became white and glistening. (Luke 9:28-29)

And it happened, as He was alone praying, that His disciples joined Him, and He asked them, saying, "Who do the crowds say that I am?" (Luke 9: 18)

Then Jesus came with them to a place called Gethsemane, and said to the disciples, "Sit here while I go and pray over there." And He took with Him Peter and the two sons of Zebedee, and He began to be sorrowful and deeply distressed. Then He said to them, "My soul is exceedingly sorrowful, even to death. Stay here and watch with Me." He went a little farther and fell on His face, and prayed, saying, "O My Father, if it is possible, let this cup pass from Me; nevertheless, not as I will, but as You wil!." Then He came to the disciples and found them asleep, and said to Peter, "What? Could you not watch with Me one hour? Watch and pray, lest you enter into temptation. The spirit indeed is willing, but the flesh is weak." Again, a second time, He went away and prayed, saying, "O My Father, if this cup cannot pass away from Me unless I drink it, Your will be done."

And He came and found them asleep again, for their eyes were heavy. So He left them, went away again, and

> *prayed the third time, saying the same words.* (Matt. 26:36-44)

> *...who, in the days of His flesh, when He had offered up prayers and supplications, with vehement cries and tears to Him who was able to save Him from death, and was heard because of His godly fear...* (Heb.5:7)

> *The disciples took note of both the constant regimen of His prayer life and the unmistakable results it produced. Now it came to pass, as He was praying in a certain place, when He ceased, that one of His disciples said to Him, "Lord, teach us to pray, as John also taught his disciples.* (Luke 11:1)

The dynamic results of His public ministry were a manifestation of the quantity and quality of His personal prayer life. He reaped in public what He sowed in private.

His disciples connected the relationship between the two and asked Him to teach them how to pray like He did. For His disciples to become men of prayer, He had to be one. For our churches to become "houses of prayer" we, as pastors, must become men (or women) of prayer first. Of course, because nothing is impossible with God; it is possible for a non-praying pastor to, by the grace of God, have a praying church.

But that will always be the exception to the rule, the rule being "Praying churches have praying pastors." The things that are important and a priority to the pastor become important and a priority to his church.

Many pastors are asked and expected to do far too much in their churches. The many hats they wear can easily exhaust the majority of their time and energy. Pastors must make their own personal prayer life a priority in their daily schedule.

Yes, we pastors must pray to set the example (modeling) for our churches, but we must also pray so that, as Christ said, *"we enter not into temptation."* There is far too much at stake for the importance and discipline of prayer to be absent from the pastor's life. Studying for a message is not quality personal prayer time.

Jesus "withdrew" from the crowds of people when He became aware of His need to be spiritually replenished. He understood that His value in ministry to the multitudes was directly associated with His time of infilling in God's presence. When He felt "empty," He either pulled himself aside or sent the people away so that He could replenish His life with God's presence and power. Though He never directed attention to His personal prayer life, the tremendous value He placed on it is unmistakably evident and clear. If prayer is important in the life of a pastor, it will become important in the church also. If Jesus felt so compelled to pray, then we as ministers, leaders and churches must also rediscover that same urgency and passion for prayer.

Our Father...Holy Is Your Name

Now it came to pass, as He was praying in a certain place, when He ceased, that one of His disciples said to Him, "Lord, teach us to pray, as John so taught his disciples."

So He said to them, "When you pray, say: Our Father in heaven, Hallowed be Your name. Your kingdom come. Your will be done On earth as it is in heaven. Give us day by day our daily bread. And forgive us our sins, For we also forgive everyone who is indebted to us. And do not lead us into temptation, But deliver us from the evil one." (Luke 11 : 1-4)

Matthew 6: 13b adds, *"For yours is the kingdom and the power and the glory forever. Amen."* The model prayer begins with the instruction to always approach our Father's throne with *worship and praise*. This prayer model is not given to us for us to mindlessly pray with vain repetition. It is a prayer outline, a format, a model. It gives us guidelines that reveal kingdom principles for us to *follow* in prayer. Our prayers are to be enveloped in praise and worship from beginning to end.

The Lord Jesus then directs us into the understanding of what prayer is to be. Your kingdom come, Your will be done on earth as it is in heaven. These two sentences contain the substantive core of what the purpose and power of prayer is designed to accomplish in the earth. *Prayer invites and initiates God's intervention into the circumstances of the world.*

Prayer changes people and things. This is what true intercession is: prayer on behalf of others that brings about the rule of Christ and the will of God. It is praying not for the eventual heavenly kingdom (the second coming of Christ), but for a present day manifestation of this glorious kingdom. "Your kingdom come, here and now!" That is the teaching and tone of this promise. Prayer releases God's will to be done on earth here and now. God has chosen the vehicle of prayer to be our primary tool for His kingdom and will to be expressed on earth. The kingdom of God advances on earth when the prayers of the church scene to heaven.

Two Arenas of Prayer

1.) Reactive Prayer

Reactive prayer is praying over and about what is needful and necessary in the life of a congregation. It is prayer requests from the life of the church. Bear one another's burdens and so fulfill the law of Christ. (Gal. 6:2)

It is a good and healthy thing that the church knows, cares and prays about the needs of its members. This "safety-net" must be an important ingredient in the prayer life of a local church. People should be comfortable and confident that if they have needs, they will be prayed over among the church. *Confess your trespasses to one another, and pray for one another, that you may be healed. The effective, fervent prayer of a righteous man avails much.* (James 5: 16)

We show true love and compassion for people when we care enough to pray for them. The church gives genuine expression of God's love for one another through prayer. Ministry, grace and life flow into and through the *local* church whose members are praying for each other.

2.) Proactive Prayer

There is absolutely nothing to be condemned in a church's having a vigorous internal prayer ministry for its members. But, if we're not careful, the entire energy and effort of prayer can be consumed by a church's internal needs. We must also add to our prayer planning and practice proactive prayer that targets objectives and outcomes outside the walls of our church.

This is the advancing of the kingdom quality of prayer: prayer for the lost to be saved, for the bound to be delivered, for our cities and nations to be transformed. Proactive prayer makes a bold stand to take more ground for the kingdom of God. The church must find a balance between these two arenas of prayer and not diminish or forsake either one.

The Apostle Paul wrote to his son in the faith, Timothy, and said: *This charge I commit unto thee, son Timothy, according to the prophecies which went before on thee, that thou by them mightest war a good warfare.* (1 Tim. 1:18)

The prophecies Timothy had received from Paul and others were given to him to reveal and confirm God's will for his life. They represented a future blueprint of what God desired to accomplish for and through Timothy's life. The Holy Spirit led Paul to challenge Timothy to take these powerful promises off the shelf and to put them to use. The Holy Spirit's instruction was for Timothy to *"wage a good warfare by your prophecies."* This was a mandate for Timothy to pray for his prophecies to become realities in his life. The unfinished ministry of his young life was to be specifically targeted in an aggressive prayer strategy. Prophecy for our lives and churches must be used proactively through prayer and intercession. Your prophecy is a weapon that, through prayer, brings about the will of God for our lives.

Praying for Pastors and Leaders

One of the greatest strategic failures of the modern church is the failure of the church to adequately cover its leaders with prayer. Did you pray for your pastor and his family today? Did anyone? I'll tell you who's been thinking, planning and working to destroy him this very day: Satan and his army. If you and your church have neglected to pray regularly, scripturally and passionately for your pastor, then you have done him (or her) a great disservice. The spiritual attack and warfare against church leaders is greater than most Christians will ever experience. As a pastor, I beg you to please pray for your pastor and other leaders.

Maybe the early church had so much success so *quickly* that they relaxed in respect to praying a prayer covering over their leaders.

> *Now about that time Herod the king stretched out his hand to harass some from the church. Then he killed James the brother of John with the sword. And because he saw that it pleased the Jews, he proceeded further to seize Peter also.*
> *Now it was during the Days of Unleavened Bread. So when he had arrested him, he put him in prison, and delivered him to four squads of soldiers to keep him, intending to bring him before the people after Passover.*

Peter was therefore kept in prison, but constant prayer was offered to God for him by the church.

And when Herod was about to bring him out, that night Peter was sleeping, bound with two chains between two soldiers; and the guards before the door were keeping the prison.

Now behold, an angel of the Lord stood by him, and a light shone in the prison; and he struck Peter on the side and raised him up, saying, "Arise quickly!"

And his chains fell off his hands.

Then the angel said to him, "Gird yourself and tie on your sandals"; and so he did. And he said to him, "Put on your garment and follow me."

So he went out and followed him, and did not know that what was done by the angel was real, but thought he was seeing a vision . When they were past the first and the second guard posts, they came to the iron gate that leads to the city, which opened to them of its own accord; and they went out and went down one street, and immediately the angel departed from him.

And when Peter had come to himself, he said, "Now I know for certain that the Lord has sent His angel, and has delivered me from the hand of Herod and from all

> *the expectation of the Jewish people."*
> *So, when he had considered this, he came to the house of Mary, the mother of John whose surname was Mark, where many were gathered together praying. And as Peter knocked at the door of the gate, a girl named Rhoda came to answer. When she recognized Peter's voice, because of her gladness she did not open the gate, but ran in and announced that Peter stood before the gate.*
> *But they said to her, "You are beside yourself!" Yet she kept insisting that it was so. So they said, "It is his angel."*
> *Now Peter continued knocking; and when they opened the door and saw him, they were astonished. (Acts 12:1-16)*

The church had just experienced the martyrdom Apostle James and the imprisonment of Apostle Peter by the hands of the demonized King Herod. They reacted quickly by forming a nonstop prayer ministry. The bible says "constant" prayer; the word includes length and intensity. It was unceasing prayer. It was fervent, intense and passionate prayer. This prayer strategy brought about the supernatural release of the Apostle from prison and from an impending death sentence.

Our leaders must have this same quality of protection through prevailing prayer over their lives. There is no greater gift you can give your pastor than to be a prayer warrior for his life and family. As a pastor, do you have a group of trusted intercessors who regularly pray for you? If the answer is yes, then praise God. If the answer is no, then please seek the Lord for this vital support. Talk to your church; seek out mature leaders; open your life to others. The Lord will help you repair this area of vulnerability and turn it into a strength in your life and church.

The Great Prayer Revival

God *is stirring* His people around the world concern*ing* prayer. Everything God promises and we, in turn, long for (salvation of souls, healing, miracles, cities and nations transformed) has *its* genesis in prayer. God's desire is for His power to increase *in* all the earth. Prayer is the generator of Gods power in the earth. Prayer will be the successful strategy that *unlocks His* power to this hurting world. I've told my congregation, I *believe* that, before very long, our doors will never be closed ever again and that twenty-four-hour prayer and worship every day of the week will become a normal part of the experience of the last-day church on earth.

Chapter Five:
Outreach

The true measure of a church's heart is not discovered by their internal love and commitment to each other. Most churches would readily describe themselves as a "loving" body of believers and they're probably right in doing so. It is good, worthy of recognition and praise, if our churches treat their fellow members in a Christ-like, loving fashion. However, though this is an admirable quality in any church, it still does not properly reflect what the true heart of the church is.

    A church's heart is revealed by how it feels and responds to those outside of its doors. A church with a healthy heart will demonstrate it by reaching out to others outside its walls. It is the real measure of God's love among us that we care about the lost and the hurting through local, regional and international outreach efforts.

    Most churches in America grow primarily from nonevangelistic influences such as transfer growth from other churches and population growth in suburban areas. There is nothing intrinsically wrong with this kind of growth by itself, but the problem it creates is that it can be a false indicator of the health and heart of a church. This kind of growth can create the appearance of a church being strong and healthy when that may not be the case at all.

A church with a healthy heart will be praying, planning and reaching out to the lost continuously. It is a natural part of the DNA of a healthy church to be passionately involved in evangelism. The absence of such passion indicates that something is missing in the very heart of the church. No matter how we attempt to justify such a conclusion, the truth is, an unevangelistic church is an unhealthy church. The diagnosis of "heart disease" in a church is a serious condition, but because it is curable it need not be terminal. The heart of a church can change. It can be repaired and restored to what God has called it to be.

Capturing the Heart of God

For the love of Christ compels us, because we judge thus: that if One died for all, then all died. (2 Cor. 5:14) The word "compels" means "to have a tight grip on." It is wonderfully true that Christ's love has an unbreakable hold on our lives. He won't let go of us or let anyone or anything pull us from the grip of His love. It is because of the secure hold his love has on us that we become controlled by its abiding influence on our life. His love becomes the most dominant influence in our lives a His children.

The Amplified Bible says it this way: *For the love of Christ controls and urges and impels us...* The Message version reads: *Christ's love has moved me to such extremes. His love has the first and last word in everything we do.* The engagement of ministry and evangelism is the byproduct of the experience of

Christ's love. It is his love that is the driving force behind mankind's redemption. *For God so loved the world that He gave His only begotten Son, that whoever believes in Him should not perish but have everlasting life.* (John 3: 16) God "so loved" the world. Everything that he has done for us was birthed in his great love for us. In the earthly ministry of Christ we clearly see the "compelling" force behind his actions.

> *Now a leper came to Him, imploring Him, kneeling down to Him and saying to Him, "If You are willing, You can make me clean." Then Jesus, moved with compassion, stretched out His hand and touched him, and said to him, "I am willing; be cleansed."* (Mark 1:40-41)

> *However, Jesus did not permit him, but said to him, "Go home to your friends, and tell them what great things the Lord has done for you, and how He has had compassion on you."* (Mark 5:19)

> *And Jesus, when He came out, saw a great multitude and was moved with compassion for them, because they were like sheep not having a shepherd. So He began to teach them many things.* (Mark 6:34)

> *And when He came near the gate of the city, behold, a dead man was being carried out, the only son of his mother; and she was a widow. And a large*

crowd from the city was with her. When the Lord saw her, He had compassion on her and said to her, "Do not weep." Then He came and touched the open coffin, and those who carried him stood still. And He said, "Young man, I say to you arise." So he who was dead sat up and began to speak. And He presented him to his mother.
(Luke 7: 12-15)

And when Jesus went out He saw a great multitude; and He was moved with compassion for them, and healed their sick. (Matt. 14: 14)

And behold, two blind men sitting by the road, when they heard that Jesus was passing by, cried out, saying, "Have mercy on us, a Lord, Son of David!" Then the multitude warned them that they should be quiet; but they cried out all the more, saying, "Have mercy on us, a Lord, Son of David!" So Jesus stood still and called them, and said, "What do you want Me to do for you?" They said to Him, "Lord, that our eyes may be opened."
   So Jesus had compassion and touched their eyes. And immediately their eyes received sight, and they followed Him. (Matt. 20:30-34)

By his example, Christ portrayed the motivation that is to direct His church in ministry -

compassion. We are to be "moved with compassion" just as our Lord was. It is his love in us that reaches out to help the hurting and save the lost. In Jesus' own teaching, he drastically emphasized God's concern for the lost.

> *Then all the tax collectors and the sinners drew near to Him to hear Him. And the Pharisees and scribes complained, saying, "This Man receives sinners and eats with them." So He spoke this parable to them, saying: "What man of you, having a hundred sheep, if he loses one of them, does not leave the ninety-nine in the wilderness, and go after the one which is lost until he finds it? And when he has found it, he lays it on his shoulders, rejoicing. And when he comes home, he calls together his friends and neighbors, saying to them, 'Rejoice with me, for I have found my sheep which was lost!' I say to you that likewise there will be more joy in heaven over one sinner who repents than over ninety-nine just persons who need no repentance.*
>
> *"Or what woman, having ten silver coins, if she loses one coin, does not light a lamp, sweep the house, and search carefully until she finds it? And when she has found it, she calls her friends and neighbors together, saying, 'Rejoice with me, for I have found the piece which I lost!' Likewise, I say to you, there is joy in the presence of the*

angels of God over one sinner who repents."

Then He said: "A certain man had two sons. And the younger of them said to his father, 'Father, give me the portion of goods that falls to me.' So he divided to them his livelihood. And not many days after, the younger son gathered all together, journeyed to a far country, and there wasted his possessions with prodigal living.

"But when he had spent all, there arose a severe famine in that land, and he began to be in want. Then he went and joined himself to a citizen of that country, and he sent him into his fields to feed swine. And he would gladly have filled his stomach with the pods that the swine ate, and no one gave him anything. But when he came to himself, he said, 'How many of my father's hired servants have bread enough and to spare, and I perish with hunger! I will arise and go to my father, and will say to him, "Father, I have sinned against heaven and before you, and I am no longer worthy to be called your son. Make me like one of your hired servants."

"And he arose and came to his father. But when he was still a great way off, his father saw him and had compassion, and ran and fell on his neck and kissed him. And the son said to him, 'Father, I have sinned against heaven and in your sight, and am no longer worthy to be called your son.'

"But the father said to his servants, 'Bring out the best robe and put it on him, and put a ring on his hand and sandals on his feet. And bring the fatted calf here and kill it, and let us eat and be merry; for this my son was dead and is alive again; he was lost and is found.' And they began to be merry.

"Now his older son was in the field. And as he came and drew near to the house, he heard music and dancing. So he called one of the servants and asked what these things meant. And he said to him, 'Your brother has come, and because he has received him safe and sound, your father has killed the fatted calf.' But he was angry and would not go in. Therefore his father came out and pleaded with him.

"So he answered and said to his father, 'Lo, these many years I have been serving you; I never transgressed your commandment at any time; and yet you never gave me a young goat, that I might make merry with my friends. But as soon as this son of yours came, who has devoured your livelihood with harlots, you killed the fatted calf for him.' And he said to him, 'Son, you are always with me, and all that I have is yours. It was right that we should make merry and be glad, for your brother was dead and is alive *again, and was lost and is found.'"* (Luke 15:1-32)

The continuous theme of these three parables is God's longing for mankind's salvation. Because one sheep is lost and unaccounted for, the Shepherd leaves the ninety-nine and He searches for the one until he finds it. Although he has ninety-nine others who were not lost his heart compelled him to seek out the missing one. His reaction to finding the lost sheep portrays God's reaction to finding lost children. The Shepherd's joy in finding his lost sheep is genuine and contagious. He is so happy that he has to share his happiness with those he loves and knows. Jesus said there is *"more joy in heaven over one sinner who repents than over ninety-nine who need no repentance."* Having God's heart for the lost means living with an abiding sense that something is missing, someone's missing.

In all three of these parables, there is the same theme: something important is missing. It is then diligently and compassionately sought after. It is later found and joyously celebrated upon recovery. The first stage is the penetrating and abiding conviction that, in spite of all that is not lost or missing, something is missing. The pursuit that evolved was a result of the passion that was aroused. Whenever the church (its leaders and its members) becomes satisfied with who is not missing, it stops being compelled into outreach for who is still not there.

The teaching of Christ leaves no doubt about God's compassionate care and concern for mankind. When the father of the prodigal son saw his son, "he had compassion and ran and fell on his neck and kissed him." The imagery of our own heavenly father's compassion for all of us is so clear. Picture the God who runs into the arms of his wayward children, who kisses them with forgiveness and acceptance, who restores everything lost in sin. He sent for the

- Best robe (our identity)
- Ring (our authority)
- Sandals (our destiny)
- Fatted calf (our prosperity)

The necessity and urgency of seeking and finding the lost is beautifully revealed in Luke 14:15-24:

> *Now when one of those who sat at the table with Him heard these things, he said to Him, "Blessed is he who shall eat bread in the kingdom of God!" Then He said to him, "A certain man gave a great supper and invited many, and sent his servant at supper time to say to those who were invited, 'Come, for all things are now ready.' But they all with one accord began to make excuses. The first said to him, 'I have bought a piece of ground, and I must go and see it. I ask you to have me excused.' And another said, 'I have bought five yoke of oxen, and I am going to test them. I ask you to have me excused.' Still another said, 'I have married a wife, and therefore I cannot come.'*
> *"So that servant came and reported these things to his master. Then the master of the house, being*

> angry, said to his servant, 'Go out quickly into the streets and lanes of the city, and bring in here the poor and the maimed and the lame and the blind.'
> "And the servant said, 'Master, it is done as you commanded, and still there is room.' Then the master said to the servant, 'Go out into the highways and hedges, and compel them to come in, that my house may be filled. For I say to you that none of those men who were invited shall taste my supper.'"

The guest list for the great supper grew larger and larger until it included all. The servant reported back to his master that "still there is room" after many had been invited to come and eat. The desire of God is manifest in the response of the master of the house. "Go out into the highways and hedges and compel them to come in, that my house may be filled." With both determination and desperation the master recommissions his servants to explore every possibility and opportunity to fill the supper table.

The master's attitude and actions are a representation of God's. The servants are a picture of the church. Hearing and feeling the driving compulsion of the master, the servants carry out his burning desire to have a full house. No matter how full the servants may have thought the house was, in the eyes of the master it wasn't full enough. Instead of surrendering to the disappointment created by those who refused to come after being invited, the master opened his heart and home to those who needed help the most. How beautifully the heart of God is seen in the master's wishes. How clearly the evangelistic mandate of the church is revealed.

Outreach

The Lord is not slack concerning His promise, as some count slackness, but is longsuffering toward us, not willing that any should perish but that all should come to repentance. (2 Pet. 3:9)

You can hear the voice of the master, "that my house may be filled," in this promise of scripture. We commonly call this next passage of scripture "the great commission". *And Jesus came and spoke to them, saying, "All authority has been given to Me in heaven and on earth. Go therefore and make disciples of all the nations, baptizing them in the name of the Father and of the Son and of the Holy Spirit, teaching them to observe all things that I have commanded you; and lo, I am with you always, even to the end of the age."* (Matt. 28:18-20)

To every people, place, city, state and nation, the church is commissioned to "Go!" The implication of Christ's telling us that He has "all authority" is that He will release His authority to us and through us in order to accomplish the mission. "With my authority I send you to the nations to proclaim My gospel."

The messianic promise of the second chapter of the Book of Psalms also reveals a continuing work of the Spirit through the prayer of the church. *I will declare the decree: The Lord has said to Me, "You are My Son, Today I have begotten You. Ask of Me, and I will give You The nations for Your inheritance, And the ends of the earth for Your possession."* (Ps.2:7-8)

It is Christ in us, His love and compassion, His faith and authority, which causes us to pray this prayer asking for the nations. The will of God becomes the prayer of the church for all the nations to be saved. Praying comes before proclaiming in the stages of evangelism. Prayer does not replace going nor does going replace prayer, but together they form the conditions that make evangelism successful. Prayer for the lost, for hearts to be softened and opened to the good news of salvation is an outreach itself When we pray for those that need salvation, we reflect the love of God for those people. It is also in this place of prayer that God envelops our hearts with a greater love for those for whom we are praying.

The church isn't always good at evangelistic strategies. We tend to be too programmed, too planned and, many times, too rigid in what should be a much more natural behavior. In helping us escape an unfruitful and religious mindset, Jesus taught us about ministry:

> *But he, wanting to justify himself, said to Jesus, "And who is my neighbor?"*
> *Then Jesus answered and said: "A certain man went down from Jerusalem to Jericho, and fell among thieves, who stripped him of his clothing, wounded him, and departed, leaving him half dead. Now by chance a certain priest came down that road. And when he saw him, he passed by on the other side. Likewise a Levite, when he arrived at the place, came and looked, and passed by on the other side. But a certain Samaritan, as he*

journeyed, came where he was. And when he saw him, he had compassion. So he went to him and bandaged his wounds, pouring on oil and wine; and he set him on his own animal, brought him to an inn, and took care of him. On the next day, when he departed, he took out two denarii, gave them to the innkeeper, and said to him, 'Take care of him; and whatever more you spend, when I come again, I will repay you.' So which of these three do you think was neighbor to him who fell among the thieves?"

And he said, "He who showed mercy on him." Then Jesus said to him, "Go and do likewise." (Luke 10:29-37)

    The parable begins with a violent assault on an innocent man. The man is stripped, wounded (traumatized) and abandoned by thieves. In describing his condition after this attack, Jesus said he was left "half dead." What a powerfully descriptive phrase for what kind of life there is without Christ. There are billions of "half dead" people who have been assaulted by the sin nature, the world's culture and Satan's powers, neither dead nor alive, imperfect and incomplete. Everyone you know and see that is not yet born again is "half dead."

    As this broken man lay bleeding and naked in the road, a priest happens to come across him. The priest was a man that had given his life in the service of God, a man that perhaps was on his very way to carry out ministerial duties and responsibilities.

What did the paid, professionally trained minister do when his life intersected that of the half-dead man? He passed by on the other side in order to avoid the injured man. On his way to do what he thought was his ministry, he passed right by someone who needed his ministry. On the way to church, his mind was closed to the real purpose of ministry. Ministry isn't something you go to do, it's what you find walking through life.

    Another religious man, a "Levite," had the same reaction as the priest when he happened on the half-dead man. In this parable, Jesus has used two of the most prominently important categories of Jewish life, a priest and a Levite. He now introduces a third man, a Samaritan. The Jews were socially and religiously very critical and condemning of the Samaritans. In fact, they had nothing to do with them if at all possible. The Samaritan "had compassion" on the hurt man. Could it be that, because of great pain in his own life, the Samaritan was most compassionate when he saw someone else in great suffering? Helping hunting people, that's what compassion looks like. That's what real ministry is all about: healing people's hurts, seeing and meeting someone's need. Ministry doesn't have to be forced or coerced. It should be the natural response of God's love in us when we encounter someone in need.

    The Samaritan had a different perspective on the hurting, half-dead man than the others who passed him by. To him, the man didn't represent a problem, a delay or a burden; to the Samaritan, the man was someone who was in real need of help. The "ministry" of the Samaritan was born out of an opportunity (the hurting man) and a mindset

(willingness both to see the need before him and then to involve himself in meeting the need.)

The world all around us is full of unlimited opportunity (multitudes of half-dead people in desperate need of God's grace and comfort) for outreach ministry. The real key for a church to become an evangelistically outreaching body of believers is in gaining the mindset of what ministry really is. Ministry is meeting people's needs. We are all called into this ministry. When a church adopts this attitude of the basic concept of ministry, the light bulb goes on in the heart and minds of the members—they are called to meet people's needs. It is there that ministry begins to flow out of the church without having to be created and controlled by the pastoral staff. The members of the church, now awakened into the meaning of ministry, begin to reach out to people in their own world. Once this mindset of ministry has been adopted by a church, ministry begins to Row automatically and spontaneously out of their lives.

Don't Be Intimidated Into Silence!

We live in a time when there's been an open hostility unleashed on many Christian ministries and churches. This is an attempt by ungodly, anti-Christ forces to intimidate the witness of the church into silence. From our pulpits we must recognize and resist any attempt to silence our voices or to stop our evangelistic mission. As the early church began to explode in numbers and influence, they were challenged and threatened in an attempt to stop their momentum. *"Now, Lord, look on their threats, and grant to Your servants that with all boldness they may speak Your word, by stretching out Your hand to heal, and that signs and wonders may be done through the name of Your holy Servant Jesus." And when they had prayed, the place where they were assembled together was shaken; and they were all filled with the Holy Spirit, and they spoke the word of God with boldness."* (Acts 4:29-31)

When the spirit of fear and intimidation came to try to silence the early church, their prayer was for boldness. The same Holy Spirit that filled the church then with boldness, will fill the church now with boldness. There is too much at stake for us to be bullied into silence. Heaven and hell are real. Eternity is real. Salvation is real and life is short. The Holy Spirit is our divine partner in ministry and evangelism. He is our enabler. He is our source of strength and boldness. *"But you shall receive power when the Holy Spirit has come upon you; and you shall be witnesses to Me in Jerusalem, and in all Judea and Samaria, and to the end of the earth."* (Acts 1:8)

The power of the Holy Spirit makes the timid to be bold, the cowardly to be courageous, the fearful to be unafraid. Through the presence and the power of the Holy Spirit, the one hundred and twenty believers that were gathered in secret in Jerusalem turned the world upside down in their lifetimes. The Holy Spirit that empowered them will empower us as we seek and yield to Him in our lives.

World Outreach:
The Local Church and Missions

Every church is called to be a missions church. Regardless of the size or particular emphasis that may define the character of a local church, each one has been included in the mandate of world evangelism. To care, pray, send and support outreaches in other lands and countries is a responsibility that is inbred into the very fabric of the Christian church. This is the core of our meaning and purpose as churches - fulfilling the great commission of Jesus Christ to "go into all the world" with His gospel. Our church, like many others, has the flags of dozens of nations hanging on our sanctuary walls. They are there to remind all of us of the commandment God's given us to reach out to those nations with the gospel and the love of Christ. We must not forget nor neglect our vital role as churches concerning world evangelism.

World Evangelism is Possible!

It is now entirely possible for the united Body of Christ to reach the entire world with the gospel of Jesus Christ. The awakening of God's desire for global evangelism in the church, coupled with the understanding of spiritual demographics realities, has propelled a fresh emphasis of world outreach.

There is a new unprecedented spirit of cooperation and unity among many different segments of the church towards the common goal of world evangelism. With the help of modern communication and travel technologies, what once only seemed like an impossible dream is suddenly an attainable hope. We are the generation that has the opportunity and the ability to see the commandment of Christ fulfilled. *"And this gospel of the kingdom will be preached in all the world as a witness to all the nations, and then the end will come."* (Matt. 24: 14)

Chapter Six: Community

No matter what initially draws people to visit or even join churches, the main reason people choose to stay in those churches is because they've found and developed valuable relationships there. This represents more than a simple demographic reality; it reveals a vitally important spiritual principal concerning one of our basic needs as human beings. We are designed to need and seek after friendship, relationship and community.

    The church is called to be much more than the impersonal dispenser of spiritual truth. We are called to be God's family and His Kingdom community in the earth. Real, lasting and life-transforming ministry flows through the spiritual law of relationship. The quality of our relationships determines the quality of ministry. To be successful in ministry, we must also be successful in relationships. Relationship is the law of ministry. Ministry flows through relationship.

    In our culture there are thousands of different expressions of our desire to experience community. Most of these various avenues are formed by people sharing a common interest or activity that in turn creates a purposeful community. Some of these groups have a valuable purpose, others a less-than-noble, or even a destructive, one. The purpose that brings people together ultimately becomes a secondary priority when the relational need is being met. Being together itself becomes as important as, or even more so than, what brings people together in the first place.

Although our primary purpose as the church remains unchanged (see chapters 1 and 4), the fact that our need for relationship and community is also satisfied is a part of God's grand plan for the church. The church has been created by God to be the most life-giving and satisfying human community in all the earth. Is there in any other group of people the same promise of wholeness, fullness and usefulness as there is in the body of Christ, the church? The church, at its scriptural best, is the greatest community in the world. God made it to be that way. That doesn't mean we have always been successful in the implementation of the great promise of His design, but it does mean the church holds the potential power to do so.

Assimilation

In church leadership circles we often speak of "closing the back door" in our churches. This is a reference to the glaring reality that most church's do not successfully assimilate into their regular membership the vast majority of their visitors. Out of this problematic reality has arisen literally hundreds of plans and programs, each seeking to solve the issue of un-successful assimilation.

If we are to find correct answers, we must first understand the real problem. When people come to a church, they're looking for a place where they can find and experience God: His love, His life, His word and His grace. Secondly, they're looking for a place where they can make friendships. The church that offers both of these solutions to their quest has the greatest opportunity for becoming the place they call home. It becomes then the challenge of the local church to create an atmosphere where both of these needs are met in people's lives.

When a visitor becomes a member or regular attendee, many times they do so in hope of finding future friendship in the church. If this hope is unrealized, it can be the singular reason for their withdrawing or outright removal from the church. The task of the church then becomes perfectly clear; we must diligently work to help create an environment and an opportunity for godly relationships and friendships to form and function in our churches.

The methods used to carry out the mission of relationship will, and do, vary from church to church, city to city, culture to culture. Whether it's in a cell group, small groups, interest groups, outreach groups, accountability groups, disciple groups or any other relational structure depends on what works best there and how the Lord leads that individual church. Once we understand the vital importance of the desire and the need for relational community, we will then give the necessary commitment to the specific strategy the Lord gives to meet it. There is no magical method or program. The method will be only .as successful as the understanding and passion of the mission. *And they continued steadfastly in the apostles' doctrine and fellowship, in the breaking of bread, and in prayers.* (Acts 2:42)

The famous Greek word for "fellowship" is *koinonia*. *Koinonia* means "communion, society, partnership, participation, unity, close association, the brotherhood, closest fellowship." The picture of *koinonia* is found in the same chapter, verses 46 - 47: *So continuing daily with one accord in the temple, and breaking bread from house to house, they ate their food with gladness and simplicity of heart, praising God and having favor with all the people. And the Lord added to the church daily those who were being saved.*

By this time, there were over 3000 members in this new, burgeoning church. In spite of their meteoric numerical growth, this was a healthy, thriving and continuingly growing church. One of the essential components of their belief and behavior was that "they continued in ... fellowship."

They had created a successful network for the purpose of fellowship. From "house to house" they not only grew in the "Apostles doctrine" but also in close fellowship and friendship with each other. The result was that the entire city of Jerusalem smiled approvingly on them and many new believers came to the Lord. The world is supposed to see something so attractive and unique in the pattern of behavior among the church that it recognizes it as the work of God. *"A new commandment I give to you, that you love one another; as I have loved you, that you also love one another. By this all will know that you are My disciples, if you have love for one another."* (John 13:34-35)

The great commandment of Christ is that we exhibit the same quality of selfless, godly and Christ-like love that Jesus modeled in His earthly ministry. We must search with great determination to be successful in truly sharing God's love with one another in the community of faith. The world is looking for a people and a place where God's love rules and reigns. That place is the church. When they see God's love in action in the life of the church, it become as powerful a witness for Christ as anything else the church can do. The word of God likens the church to a physical body.

> *For as the body is one and has many members, but all the members of that one body, being many, are one body, so also is Christ. For by one Spirit we were all baptized into one body-whether Jews or Greeks, whether slaves or free- and have all been made to drink into one Spirit. For in fact the body is not one member but many. If the foot should say, "Because I am not a hand, I am not of the body," is it therefore not of the body? And if the ear should say, "Because I am not an eye, I am not of the body," is it therefore not of the body? If the whole body were an eye, where would be the hearing? If the whole were hearing, where would be the smelling? But now God has set the members, each one of them, in the body just as He pleased. And if they were all one member, where would the body be? But now indeed there are many members, yet one body. And the eye cannot say to the hand, "I have no need of you"; nor again the head to the feet, "I have no need of you." No, much*

rather, those members of the body which seem to be weaker are necessary. And those members of the body which we think to be less honorable, on these we bestow greater honor; and our unpresentable parts have greater modesty, but our presentable parts have no need. But God composed the body, having given greater honor to that part which lacks it, that there should be no schism in the body, but that the members should have the same care for one another. And if one member suffers, all the members suffer with it; or if one member is honored, all the members rejoice with it. Now you are the body of Christ, and members individually. (1 Cor. 12:12-27)

    The first part of this same chapter of scripture deals with the explanation of spiritual gifts. The following metaphor of "the body" is given to help us see the interconnectedness of our lives to each other. Just as our physical bodies have many different members, the body of Christ (the church) has many different members. By the great design of God, our physical bodies are a beautiful picture of the connection and cooperation of many different members that form one body. The value of our physical members is in their relationship to the rest of the body. If any member is "cut off" from the body, that member has no use or benefit. Its value is in its attachment to and function with the rest of the body.
    In the body of Christ, there are no useless or unessential members. Every person in the body of

Christ has meaning, purpose, value and significance for the rest of the body. God has made it to be that way. The church is the place where people discover and display their own unique giftedness. Every single member in the church has an important, irreplaceable ministry. The church becomes healthy, strong and Christ revealing when its members are functioning in their ministries. Once again the scriptures portray the church as a body in the following passage:

> *And He Himself gave some to be apostles, some prophets, some evangelists, and some pastors and teachers, for the equipping of the saints for the work of ministry, for the edifying of the body of Christ, till we all come to the unity of the faith and of the knowledge of the Son of God, to a perfect man, to the measure of the stature of the fullness of Christ; that we should no longer be children, tossed to and fro and carried about with every wind of doctrine, by the trickery of men, in the cunning craftiness of deceitful plotting, but, speaking the truth in love, may grow up in all things into Him who is the head - Christ - from whom the whole body, joined and knit together by what every joint supplies, according to the effective working by which every part does its share, causes growth of the body for the edifying of itself in love. (Eph. 4:11-16)*

The ministry gifts (apostle, prophet, evangelist, pastor and teacher) are the God-anointed and ordained equipping agents of the church. Their work is in preparing, training, perfecting and restoring God's people. Then those who have been equipped are called to do the work of ministry, for the edifying of the body of Christ. We are called to grow up in all things as the body of Christ. When that happens, every member contributes - every joint supplies, according to the effective working by which every part does its share. When that happens the body grows and edifies itself created both to be needed and to need one another in the Body of Christ. This is a process that requires great commitment and patience. It demands that we stay involved in the process and not abandon it even if we're hurt or disappointed in it.

Pain, misunderstanding, offense and discouragement are all part of the reality of human relationships. They will also (regrettably so) be a part of the building of community and covenant in the church. But just like a marriage that has overcome its struggles and setbacks to then become strong and Christ honoring, the church must make that kind of quality commitment to each other to work through their different issues. The level of personal commitment a believer makes to be an active member in the body of Christ, ultimately determines the result. It takes a great commitment to produce a great result. The less the individual commitment, the less the value of the experience in both giving and receiving in the church. The church is worth believing in and committing to.

Rebuilding a Sense of Community

In my area (Phoenix, Arizona), there is tremendous population flux and transition. Lots of people both move here and move away from here. The average home owner moves every two and half years. One of the net results of such severe demographic movement is a lack of true community. In the culture of this region, there is reservation and even resistance to forming the structures of a community. Politicians and other cultural leaders all agree there's a problem. These same negative dynamics also affect the church world. Even though there are reasonable explanations for this pervasive problem, the church here must overcome these barriers and work to build strong relationships. We have no other choice.

In your area there may be a different set of conditions that have contributed to the absence of relational strength and community. No matter what those various constructs may be, we must lead our churches out of these *controlling* influences into the pattern of the scriptures. There is no replacement for relationship and community. The great promise of all the church is called to be is dependent on the presence and power of relational community.

Our society and cultures are being ravaged by the pain created by broken covenants. Marriage itself is under all-out attack from the enemy. As people come into the church from broken homes, they are in desperate need of healing and grace. The depth of the ministry they need requires building successful relationship in order to successfully minister to them.

Many people that have been hurt in their family or other relationships are genuinely hesitant and fearful about entering into close fellowship with others. The church must be consistently compassionate in reaching out to those who hurt the most. We must be understanding and patient as these precious lives come out of their darkness. We must be lovingly persistent in helping people to open their lives up to one another in the church. We also must give people their "space and time" until they're able to enter into close fellowship and community. As we model the workings and rewards of community in the church, we invite others to be a part of this life-giving fellowship.

Discipleship, Mentoring, Coaching and Training

At the core of the purpose of the church is the command to make disciples of all the nations (Matt. 28: 19). This inescapable mandate must be at the center of our plans, purposes, goals and activities as churches. We exist as churches in order to fulfill the will of God in regard to His desire for the making of disciples. Although in His earthly ministry Jesus Christ ministered to great multitudes, He personally mentored a much smaller group of people. Jesus chose twelve men that He befriended and mentored for three years. As the book of Acts begins, we find there are 120 committed followers and Disciples of Christ awaiting the promise of the Holy Spirit in the upper room in Jerusalem.

After all the betrayal, violence, disappointment and confusion that erupted after the crucifixion of Christ, a great separation followed. Tens of thousands of people had experienced the healing, preaching and miracle ministry of Christ during the preceding three years. The tremendous demonstration of power, love and revelation through His ministry had created a huge following. Although they readily recognized and celebrated the great things He did, they never truly knew who He was. At the end, only the relatively small group of people that had a strong, personal relationship with Jesus remained. This remnant of 120 true disciples of Christ literally changed the world in their lifetime. The size and influence of the church grew exponentially throughout the world through the ministry of this small band of disciples of Jesus Christ.

Real discipleship requires real relationship. Jesus knew this and committed the time and effort necessary to impart His life unto others. His model for mentoring disciples serves as an example of the value of building relationships for the purpose of discipleship. He didn't teach a class called "Discipleship 101"; everything He did imparted His nature unto the men He had called. Discipleship happened with a natural ease and grace because it flowed through the relationships He had built with all these men. The success of discipleship was a result of the success of the relationships. The disciples were so comfortably secure in their relationship with Christ that they'd ask Him questions and interact with Him as friends.

Taking the lead from modern educational models and methods, we've developed an impersonal pattern of discipleship in the church. The simple dispensing of information *is* not the full picture of what discipleship is meant to be. People need to be "coached" and supported by caring friendships in order to be properly developed. Without relationships and community, discipleship becomes a difficult goal to attain. Sure, some will be able to overcome the lack of godly relationships and leadership, but many others will not be able to survive the many difficulties that relation-less discipleship creates. The Apostle Paul addressed this problem when he said, *"I do not write these things to shame you, but as my beloved children I warn you. For though you might have ten thousand instructors in Christ, yet you do not have many fathers; for in Christ Jesus I have begotten you through the gospel. Therefore I urge you, imitate me."* (1 Cor. 4:14-16)

    Do fathers give instructions? Of course they do, but fathers are much more than just instructors. There is an unbreakable relational bond between a father and his children. It is the heart of a father to see his children succeed in life. The Apostle Paul had a lovingly intimate relationship with the people in the church at Corinth. That relationship gave him access to a continuing work of discipleship with them even though he was physically absent. Paul's commitment and passion for their success was more than that of an instructor. His relationship with them created a great concern in his heart for them. With this quality mentorship, he successfully brought about great change and maturity in the church at Corinth. Discipleship was successful because relationship was successful.

Mending Nets

When He had gone a little farther from there, He saw James the son of Zebedee, and John his brother, who also were in the boat mending their nets. (Mark 1:19) The Greek word for "mending" is *katarizo*. Its several definitions include: "to repair, restore, put something in its appropriate position, equip, arrange; used in classical Greek for a doctor setting a bone during surgery; training, perfecting, preparing." The root word is used in Eph. 6: 12 for the equipping of the saints.

Picture the church as a large fishing net like the one the early disciples used. Every thread of the rope must be in place for success in fishing. The disciples were mending their nets so their efforts could succeed. Our individual lives form the great net of what the church is called to be when we are properly connected to one another through Christ-honoring relationships. We form the "net" that evangelism, discipleship and care move through in the church. When relationships are broken, the net becomes incomplete.

There is safety in belonging to the net by having several different points of relational connection to other people. If and when we personally are in need of a "safety net" of caring and healing friendships, they are already there for us. In the community of the church, there is a great protective network of interconnected lives, all caring for each other. The ministry of "mending nets" is the work of Jesus Christ the leadership of the church in healing broken lives and equipping them for their kingdom destiny as the people of God.

Brethren, if a man is overtaken in any trespass, you who are spiritual restore such a one in a spirit of gentleness, considering yourself lest you also be tempted. Bear one another's burdens, and so fulfill the law of Christ. (Gal. 6: 1-2) "Restore" is the same Greek word *katarizo*. Because the net is bound together, it is many times stronger as a whole than any of the individual threads. The weight that it lifts is distributed equally to all the many strands of rope. When we are connected to each other we can "bear one another's" burdens so that no one is improperly overwhelmed by the weight of their problems. This is the scriptural "net" of fellowship, relationship and community at work.

When a person is "overtaken in trespass," their life has been torn away from the net of fellowship with God and man. Now gripped by the deception of sinfulness, their life is in the place of damage because of the effects of their actions. But if they have established godly relationships with others in the life of the church, the ties they have can now minister a restoring grace to their life. Their brokenness can be mended if they're in the net of caring relationships. The importance and value of taking the time to develop those relationships is now paying off in a support system that brings healing to their life.

Without this safety net in place, what would happen to the life in question? Who will race to his aid? Who will fight for his soul against the temptation of the enemy? Who will bear his burdens? Relationship gives the opportunity for restoration to take place. Many times it's the strength of the relationship that determines the success of the restoration.

Power of Unity

In the early church, just before the great outpouring of the Holy Spirit, the Bible describes the environment that attracts God's presence and power. *These all continued with one accord in prayer and supplication, with the women and Mary the mother of Jesus, and with His brothers. (Acts 1: 14) When the Day of Pentecost had fully come, they were all with one accord in one place. And suddenly there came a sound from heaven, as of a rushing mighty wind, and it filled the whole house where they were sitting.*

Then there appeared to them divided tongues, as of fire, and one sat upon each of them. And they were all filled with the Holy Spirit and began to speak with other tongues, as the Spirit gave them utterance. (Acts 2: 1-4) The Greek word translated as "one accord" here is *homothumadon*, "having one mind and purpose; to be in agreement; group unity; to be unanimous." Their unity attracted God's great blessing and also helped them keep it.

So continuing daily with one accord in the temple, and breaking bread from house to house, they ate their food with gladness and simplicity of heart. (Acts 2:46) What they received through unity they also maintained through unity. Having one mind and purpose allowed the early church to experience truly miraculous results. When a local church has one mind and purpose, they will attract God's favor and blessing and see miraculous results also. The early church, knowing of and seeing the tremendous value of unity, refused to move away from it. Thus the momentum of God's work in their midst was never broken through division.

The vision of a local church is the rallying place for corporate unity. When there is a disagreement with the vision, there will be division. Satan works endlessly to bring division into a church in order to weaken and destroy the work of God through unity there. There is power in unity; division robs the church of its power.

The greatest way to hurt or weaken a local church is to cause division in the leadership. If the leaders can find a way to work through their differences and minister in unity, they can, for the most part, shut Satan out of their local church. When there is real unity at the top (in leadership), it flows down to the rest of the body. A husband and wife that enter into and maintain unity in their marriage *will* have blessing and authority there. The same is true for the leadership of the church.

Now the whole earth had one language and one speech ... And the Lord said, "Indeed the people are one and they all have one language, and this is what they begin to do; now nothing that they propose to do will be withheld from them." (Gen. 11:1,6) As the Lord beheld the united purpose and language of mankind He said, "Nothing they purpose to do will be withheld from them." Because of their unity of mind and speech, their potential power was enormous. (The Lord created Babel - confusion - by creating many different languages in order to stop their sinful agenda.)

There is power in unity.

> *Behold, how good and how pleasant it is*
> *For brethren to dwell together in unity!*
> *It is like the precious oil upon the head,*
> *Running down on the beard,*
> *The beard of Aaron,*
> *Running down on the edge of his garments.*
> *It is like the dew of Hermon,*
> *Descending upon the mountains of Zion;*
> *For there the Lord commanded the blessing -*
> *Life forevermore.*
> (Ps. 133: 1-3)

Unity is good! Unity attracts the anointing. Unity flows from top to bottom (leadership to others). God commands a blessing where there is unity: life evermore.

"Again I say to you that if two of you agree on earth concerning anything that they ask, it will be done for them by My Father in heaven. For where two or three are gathered together in My name, I am there in the midst of them." (Matt. 18:19-20) In this passage of scripture, Jesus was teaching about governmental actions in church leadership covering disciplinary issues. He closes this teaching with a dynamic principle of kingdom power. Agreement is power.

There is a special anointing of the presence and power of the Lord Jesus Christ when the ecclesia, His church, is gathered together. When the church, beginning with its leadership, is in agreement, they have great authority to release God's will and kingdom in the earth.

The word "agree" is *sumphoneo* in Greek. Our English word "symphony" comes from this word. It means "to be in harmony, to sound together, to be in agreement." It is a beautiful symphony in the ears of God when His church is in agreement.

When the church *truly* recognizes the great power that unity and agreement have in their lives, it *will* awaken a *resolve* to achieve it, no matter what it costs. The real Lord's Prayer is found in John 17:20-23:

> *"I do not pray for these alone, but also for those who will believe in Me through their word; that they all may be one, as You, Father, are in Me, and I in You; that they also may be one in Us, that the world may believe that You sent Me. And the glory which You gave Me I have given them, that they may be one just as We are one: I in them, and You in Me; that*

they may be made perfect in one, and that the world may know that You have sent Me, and have loved them as You have loved Me."

Chapter Seven:
Communication

Communication is power. Thousands of companies pay billions of dollars each year in order to communicate their message about their products and services to potential customers. Ad agencies are constantly creating and refining advertising models and methods in an attempt to communicate those messages more successfully. We live in a time that demographers are referring to as "the information age." Never in human history has there been so much information available to so many people. Modern technology has created an explosion of vast communication channels pouring out an unprecedented amount of information into all of our lives.

When I was a child, our television received five channels. Now we have access to hundreds of channels through cable and satellite technologies. Cell phones have brought tremendous change into the way our culture communicates. The Internet has literally put the world at our fingertips.

What does all this mean to our churches? Where is our place in relationship to the tremendous advances made in the world of communications? Is it a blessing or a curse that we live in these realities? Should we be actively engaged in the many different and expanding forms of communication that are all around us?

The Church is in the Communication Business

Communication is power and the communication of the living word of Jesus Christ unveils the very power of God to mankind. *For I am not ashamed of the gospel of Christ, for it is the power of God to salvation for everyone who believes, for the Jew first and also for the Greek.* (Rom. 1:6) The Greek word for "gospel" is evangelion, which means "good news." The presentation of the "good news" of Jesus Christ releases the power of salvation to anyone who hears and believes the message that the salvation that Christ has purchased with His precious blood is available to all mankind. It has been left to the church to communicate that great salvation for the entire world. God himself has made it to be that way.

> *For the Scripture says, "Whoever believes on Him will not be put to shame." For there is no distinction between Jew and Greek, for the same Lord over all is rich to all who call upon Him. For "whoever calls on the name of the LORD shall be saved."*
>
> *How then shall they call on Him in whom they have not believed? And how shall they believe in Him of whom*

they have not heard? And how shall they hear without a preacher? And how shall they preach unless they are sent? As it is written: "How beautiful are the feet of those who preach the gospel of peace, who bring glad tidings of good things!" (Rom. 10:11-15)

Paul lays out five things that go into communicating the "good news":

1. Someone must be sent.
2. They must preach the good news of Christ.
3. They must go so others can hear.
4. After hearing, they will believe.
5. Because they believe, they will call on Jesus.

All Christians are ordained to be evangels, those who herald the good news of Jesus Christ. At the very center of the created mission of the church is the great responsibility to tell the whole world about what Jesus has done for them! Salvation itself becomes dependent on the quantity and quality of the communication expertise of the church.

Beautiful Feet

I don't know about you, but I don't have what could be accurately described as "beautiful feet." My feet are big, many of my toes broken and injured in high school and college sports. The reference to having beautiful feet is not a reference to having a pedicure; it's a historical reference to an ancient form of communication. When nations and their armies battled in war, they would use runners to carry important messages from the battlefield back to the kings and leaders. When a messenger brought back good news because of a great military victory, his feet were considered beautiful. The method of communication (runners) was described as "beautiful" because of the power of the message.

The Method is not Sacred—the Message Is

Jesus continually changed the methodology of His earthly ministry. He used many different ways to heal the sick (laying on of hands, speaking the word only, spitting on them, sending them to the priest, touching his clothes, and so on). He used many different arenas to preach the gospel (seaside, mountain top, temple, house, and so forth). He used many different illustrations and metaphors in His preaching and teaching about the kingdom of God Why all the variety?

1. Because we have a tendency to put undeserved sacredness on methods. The great bronze serpent Moses had made that healed and delivered the children of Israel eventually became an object of religious idolatry (2 Kings 18:4). The method is not sacred, the message is.

2. Secondly, variety is an expression of the great creativity of our God. Ministry should also exhibit the creative ability of God working in His church.

3. Thirdly, the church must be sensitive to finding the appropriate method of ministry and communication for the intended audience they're called to reach. To be unbending in methodology will limit the effectiveness of ministry.

Is Rock-and-Roll from the Devil?
When I was a young boy in the sixties and early seventies, the majority of the churches had a knee-jerk reaction to that "new music" called rock-and-roll. Preacher after preacher used their pulpits to condemn the music that they were so sure came directly out of hell itself. Now, I agree that music can be demonic, but to resist the cultural expression of changing musical tastes was a major mistake. Now those same Christian denominations have guitars and drum sets on their stages and sing worship songs that have a rock-and-roll rhythm. Musical styles are a simple matter of personal preference and taste. There is no style of music that is more anointed or better suited for ministry and worship. The method (style of music) is not sacred, the message is.

Music becomes beautiful when it connects its message and meaning to the hearer. All ministry is the same. In the ears of the hearer, the method by which the truth has come to them is beautiful because it resulted in salvation. The ancient runner's ugly feet became beautiful to the lives of those he carried good news to.

Can You Hear Me Now?
There are mountains in and around the metropolitan Phoenix area where I live and pastor. In certain places where I drive, the cell-phone signal is weak or even broken by those geographical challenges. Calls have to be redialed in order for the conversation to continue. Have you ever talked on and on to someone who wasn't even connected on the other end of the phone? It takes a successful connection to achieve successful communication.

Truth Doesn't Set You Free Until You Know It.

Then Jesus said to those Jews who believed Him, "If you abide in My word, you are My disciples indeed. And you shall know the truth, and the truth shall make you free." (John 8:31-32)

The truth doesn't set you free; the truth you know sets you free. The mission of the church is to make God's truth known. Every possible method and device that can help facilitate that mission must be successfully incorporated into our church strategies and activities.

Truth has the power to set mankind free. The church has the privilege to make truth known. Any and all methods of communication that can be used to dispense the truth of God's word should be used.

Goliath's Sword

So David prevailed over the Philistine with a sling and a stone, and struck the Philistine and killed him. But there was no sword in the hand of David. Therefore David ran and stood over the Philistine, took his sword and drew it out of its sheath and killed him, and cut off his head with it. And when the Philistines saw that their champion was dead, they fled. (1 Sam. 17:50-51)

David used the weapon he was skilled and experienced with to render Goliath unconscious. With a sling and a stone, a rag and a rock, David brought Goliath down. But to finish the job of killing Goliath and removing his huge head, he lacked weaponry for there was no sword in his hand. Instead of returning back to the armies of Israel with an incomplete outcome, he gained inspiration and creativity to think outside the box. He took away the enemy's own weapon that had been used to destroy and oppress Israel for decades. When he reached down and pulled that gigantic sword out of its sheath, he redeemed and sanctified it for God's purpose in the earth.

The sword itself was used for good or bad depending on the hand that wielded it. The same weapon that had previously shed innocent blood was now used by David to bring about an unprecedented historical victory for an entire nation. He used a worldly weapon for a spiritual victory that gave validity to the unusual means and method used to achieve it. The same weaponry that has brought defilement and devastation to our culture can and must be redeemed by the hands of the church. Television, radio, the Internet, movies, books, music, arts, billboards, and so on, have all been used to propagate and promote anti-Christian messages in our world. That's because they've been in the hands of the ungodly. These same instruments of communication can be redeemed by the church to be used as great tools of salvation, healing, hope and deliverance to a lost world.

Internal Communication

How a church develops and achieves successful internal communication is very important.

1.) The message must be clear. Confusion is the product of unsuccessful communication. Whatever we are attempting to communicate (a sermon, an announcement, a building program, an evangelistic outreach or anything else) must be communicated as simply and precisely as possible.

2.) It must be communicated repeatedly. Saying it or putting it in the church bulletin once should not be considered successful communication. The more a message is repeated, the better it' remembered.

3.) It must be communicated in different ways. Pulpit, bulletin, video announcements, mailers, websites, phone calls. The more of these that you use to make your message known, the greater he outcome will be.

4.) It should be done with excellence. Every attempt at communication conveys a message. If the bulletin is ugly and unprofessional, it sends a signal to those who read it. Excellence is not just a matter of money, it is demonstrated by preparation and appearance also. If the method is messy, unprepared and unprofessional, many times the message is lost.

5.) Communication must be bilateral in a church. Many pastors lead their churches the same way some Christians pray (engaging in a one-sided conversation, telling God everything they need and want Him to do and nothing more.) Frequently pastors and church leaders become isolated from the realities of their members because they're cut off from necessary dialogue and feedback. Healthy communication demands that communication works both ways between pastor and church members.

6.) Communication must come from a unified voice of church leaders. My wife and I have been granted the great privilege of having and raising four beautiful children. One thing I've noticed about all of my kids, especially when they were little, is they seem to have been born with degrees in psychology. Let me explain. When they would ask me a question, they would use whatever information I gave them in a follow-up interview with their mother. If Mary and I were not in total agreement with each other, they would pick that up and use it as a tool for leveraging their agenda. Mary and I soon learned that we had to make decisions together in agreement in order to survive our little "psychologists." When we were in unity, the issue was quickly settled.

When church leaders share their vision and message in agreement and unity, it communicates strength and security to the entire church. When a leader says something like, "Well, this is what pastor thinks is right to do," or expresses disagreement or displeasure with the pastor's message in any other way, s/he is attempting to sabotage that message. Pastors must work to secure unity in their leadership in order to assure the success of the communication to the entire church.

The Four Laws of Public Ministry

When I was a freshman in Bible, college I had the real privilege of attending the Church on the Way with Pastor Jack Hayford. The combination of my being eighteen years old and very impressionable and Pastor Hayford's dynamic pulpit skills, which are very impressive, created an interesting outcome. Because the church was experiencing tremendous growth that required multiple Sunday services, Pastor Hayford sometimes sat on a stool to alleviate fatigue caused by prolonged standing.

Now, at that time in my life I was in very good physical condition. I played on the college basketball team and ran ten miles every day. When my turn came to speak in homiletics class, I brought with me a stool to sit on. Sitting on that stool and using my best Hayfordesque vocabulary, I attempted to be someone I wasn't. When it was over, the class and teacher weren't too critical in their evaluations, but I knew something was wrong. I wondered about my calling altogether.

In brokenness I went to the Lord to ask Him about that fiasco I had presented. What He said to me helped and healed me. He simply said, "Son, you are not Jack Hayford." Well, I had come to that startling realization myself because of the reaction in my own heart to my homiletics failure. If that were all He had said to me, it would have helped me but not healed me. Next He said, "And, Son, Jack Hayford is not Mike Maiden." The Lord was encouraging me as a young minister to be myself Every pastor and minister must find his or her own voice in order to truly be effective in ministry.

It was during that beginning time that the Lord gave me these four simple law for public ministry: information, inspiration, application and demonstration.

Law 1: Information
Study to shew thyself approved unto God, a workman that needeth not to be ashamed, rightly dividing the word of truth. (2 Tim. 2: 15) God honors pursuit with understanding. The degree of our pursuit determines the degree of our understanding. The

degree of our understanding determines the degree of our success in ministry,

The life of a minister is an unending education. There is no substitute for preparation and study in public ministry. TheHoly Spirit blesses preparation. It is incumbent in the life of a minister to be motivated to self-educate. There are so many resources available now for study and education for ministers. Being charismatic or Pentecostal does not mean we should be intellectually indifferent or lazy. Jesus said, *"Blessed are the meek, for they shall inherit the earth."* (Matt. 5:5) If we are teachable, our destiny is reachable. We must learn to learn. If we do, the reward is the fulfillment of God's will for our lives.

Then He said to them, "Therefore every scribe instructed concerning the kingdom of heaven is like a householder who brings out of his treasure things new and old." (Matt. 13:52) This is the portrait of ministry. New and old things are together in the treasury of the minister's ministry and understanding. These should both be present in our lives as men and women of God.

Law 2: Inspiration

...who also made us sufficient as ministers of the new covenant, not of the letter but of the Spirit; for the letter kills, but the Spirit gives life. (2 Cor. 3:6) The expectation for New Testament ministry is that there will be both study and preparation in God's word and prayerfulness. The uninspired, unanointed and unpraying delivery of God's word is not what is needed to experience the results God has promised and what the early church has modeled. Our lives should be saturated with the penetrating power of the

Holy Spirit before we rise to deliver God's word to God's people.

...But His word was in my heart like a burning fire Shut up in my bones; I was weary of holding it back, And I could not. (Jer. 20:9b) We must have the fire of the Holy Spirit burning in us when we minister in the church. Jesus said, *"It is the Spirit who gives life; the flesh profits nothing. The words that I speak to you are spirit, and they are life."* (John 6:63)

The anointing of the Holy Spirit must saturate our souls as we endeavor to minister to others. Without the spark of inspiration in the delivery of God's word, the congregation is robbed of a greater measure of truth, grace and power. Passive, dispassionate and uninspired ministry is not what is needed for the miraculous results God has promised us. It is *"...not by might nor by power, but by My Spirit,"* Says the LORD of hosts. (Zech. 4:6)

We have the obligation as pastors and leaders to be continuously filled with the Holy Spirit. People may not always know the difference in our ministries when we're not "prayed up" and "spirit-filled," but God does. We must not trust in our own devices and gifts. We must look to and lean on the precious Holy Spirit who will always graciously fill us if we seek and surrender to Him.

Law 3: Application

How does what I teach or preach find a practical application in the life of those who hear me? We must constantly ask ourselves this question as we prepare to embark into any ministry in the church. This thoughtfulness requires us to put ourselves in the hearers' place.

So the Spirit lifted me up and took me away, and I went in bitterness, in the heat of my spirit; but the hand of the LORD was strong upon me. Then I came to the captives at Tel Abib, who dwelt by the River Chebar and I sat where they sat, and remained there astonished among them seven days. (Ezek. 3:14-15) Ezekiel had had one of the most remarkable spiritual experiences a human being can ever have. He was taken into the very throne room of God (chapter 1) and saw unbelievably glorious things there. Then the Lord gave him a powerful prophetic word for the nation of Israel. His heart burned with passion to speak the word to the backslidden people of Israel. But there was one more stage in his preparation for public ministry. The Lord took him down to where the captives lived by the river. Ezekiel's own description of the experience is found in the words, "I sat where they sat." Before he was released to minister a word to the people of Israel, he was required to experience the pain they were enduring. Ministry that does not identify and relate to those being ministered to will always be ineffective and incomplete. Successful ministry brings people to the place of real change in their lives.

So the people asked him, saying, "What shall we do then?"...Then tax collectors also came to be baptized, and said to him, "Teacher, what shall we do?"... Likewise the soldiers asked him, saying, "And what shall we do?" So he said to them, liDo not intimidate anyone or accuse falsely, and be content with your wages." (Luke 3:10,12,14) Leading people up to, and then showing them how to experience, change in their lives is the definition of successful leadership. Truth without a related practical application creates frustration and disappointment.

Law 4: Demonstration

Christianity was never meant to only be told: it must also be shown. As ministers and believers, we must dare to believe and expect to see the miraculous in our ministries and churches. There is an inner thirst for the supernatural in the heart of every human being. Our Creator forms this desire. When the church becomes void of the genuine demonstration of the power of God, it does a disservice and harm to the will of God in the earth. *For the kingdom of God is not in word but in power.* (1 Cor. 4:20) *And my speech and my preaching were not with persuasive words of human wisdom, but in demonstration of the Spirit and of power, that your faith should not be in the wisdom of men but in the power of God.* (1 Cor. 2:4-5; Emphasis mine) The Corinthians weren't interested in Paul's teachings until they had experienced God's power. If we give God the opportunity, He will manifest His power in our churches.

The ministry of Jesus Christ is beautifully summarized in Matt. 4:23: *Jesus went about all Galilee, teaching in their synagogues, preaching the gospel of the kingdom, and healing all kinds of sickness and all kinds of disease among the people.* Teaching, preaching and healing - the first two without the third is an expression of incomplete Christian ministry. One miracle communicates more than a hundred sermons. Just as teaching and preaching are examples of communication, so are healing and miracles. God wants His church to believe in the manifestation of His power in their midst.

"And these signs will follow those who believe: In My name they will cast out demons; they will speak with new tongues; they will take up serpents;

and if they drink anything deadly, it will by no means hurt them; they will lay hands on the sick, and they will recover."... And they went out and preached everywhere, the Lord working with them and confirming the word through the accompanying signs. (Mark 16:17-18, 20) The power of God is always available to confirm the word of God when it is taught or preached under the anointing.

External Communication

Does your city know about your church? What and how much do they know? Is your church involved in an extensive outreach to your city in order to tell them who and what you are? What is the message your church is telling your city? What does the city think about your church?

1.) Don't assume the people in your city know more about you than what you've told them.
If we want people to know who we are and what we're doing as churches, we must tell them. To most people the church is a mystery that they just don't know much about. It is our responsibility to properly introduce ourselves to them.

2.) The appearance of your church property is communicating something to your community. Churches should be well kept and inviting to those who live near or drive by them. The physical appearance of both the outside and the inside of a church is telling your community much about what kind of church you are. Churches that are run down and unkempt are speaking volumes to your neighborhood, as are churches that are beautifully maintained. The inside appearance of a church is also vitally important. First impressions communicate a message when people come to your church. It doesn't always take only money to express excellence in a church facility. We should do the best we can with what we have. People appreciate excellence in appearance and presentation.

3.) Tell your city about the good qualities of your church and ministry.
That that communication of thy faith may become effectual by the acknowledging of every good thing which is in you in Christ Jesus. (Philem. 6) Effectively communicate the good things that are a part of your church. Understand and then express to your community the positive and exceptional traits of your church. If you have a great children's ministry, then everyone in your city ought to know that. If you have exceptional musical worship, do all you can to tell that to your city. Find and focus on the strengths of your church and your ministry. Then emphasize this strengths to your community through every possible avenue. Don't let someone tell your story for you. Take the initiative to be the teller of your own story to your city.

4.) Be creative with the method and the messages you communicate.
We are competing for the attention of people that are being bombard d with advertising, images and messages. The way we communicate to them must be creative enough to have a chance to be heard and seen. There are also many media companies that specialize in helping churches communicate their message professionally. Think out of the box about

the means and messages of communicating your church's story.

5.) Know whom you're trying to reach and target your communication efforts accordingly.
The more specific the message, the more successful the communication. Sometimes in an attempt to reach everyone, we end up reaching no one. A different approach is necessary when we are looking to reach different demographic groups. If we are confident about whom we're called to minister to, then we can formulate a specific and direct strategy of communication to them. This will greatly increase the positive results of advertising and communication.

6.) Keep telling your story.
If your church has prayerfully chosen direct mailing as your primary advertising commitment, then do it repeatedly and consistently. Before people go to a store, visit a restaurant or buy some other product, they usually have had multiple exposures to that product in advertising. By the time they finally respond, they've been saturated with information that has eventually produced a decision to act. In whatever areas you invest to tell your story, be committed and consistent.

7.) Seek the Lord for wisdom and the finances required to tell your story.
God wants you to succeed. He wants your church to grow and its influence to increase in your city. He's on your side. Everything you need to be successful is available to you from your loving heavenly Father. Ask Him for the plan and He'll give it. Believe Him for the finances and He'll provide all you need. Don't let

discouragement about present problems or disillusionment about past failures stop you from believing God and moving forward. God has a plan for you and your church. His plan will work. He will provide all the finances for His plan.

Chapter Eight: Worship

Right now, across the entire world, the greatest explosion of praise and worship the earth has ever known is taking place. The church is in the middle of the greatest revival of worship it has ever known. This is much more than just a contemporary trend or a popular fad that will soon give way to something else. This is a genuine, recognizable movement of God's spirit in the hearts of His children. This is a true spiritual awakening that carries with it tremendous importance. Every time there is a major movement of God in the earth, it is always accompanied with worship.

- The creation of the world was accompanied by the symphony of angelic worship. (Job 38:4-7)

- When the son of God, Jesus Christ, the Savior of the world, was born, worship erupted from heaven. (Luke 2:8-14)

- The outpouring of the Holy Spirit on the early church brought with it a new depth of worship to mankind. (Acts 2:1-4,11)

- The atmosphere for the second coming of Christ is being created by an explosion of worship in the earth.

In the tabernacle of Moses, the altar of incense sat at the doorway between the Holy Place and the Holy of Holies, the place where God's presence dwelt. In the Holy Place, the priest would fulfill his duties and carry out His ministry. One duty was to offer up incense on the altar of incense. That fragrance would fill both rooms - the Holy Place and the Holy of Holies.
    The incense is symbolic of worship filling earth and heaven. Worship fills our lives with the fragrance of God and it then it fills His throne room with our love. As our worship fills the earth it, is creating the throne our loving king will sit on.
    This great awakening of worship is happening in every segment of Christendom. Churches that would not describe themselves as Charismatic or Pentecostal are now openly and joyously singing worship songs that come from Charismatic churches. The desire in the church world for real and intimate worship is unmistakably present in most of the body of Christ. This is an undeniable signal that something great is about to happen: the coming of Christ, the rapture of the church, the day of the Lord.

Worship Reveals the Health of the Church

The worship of a church manifests in its heart and in its health. The instrumental and vocal components of worship are not what ultimately determine its success and quality. True worship flows from our hearts.

Healthy churches exhibit vibrant, joyous and passionate worship not only because they have been taught about the "how-tos" of worship but, more important, because worship reveals who we really are, not just what we do, to God.

Worship Changes Peoples Lives

Nothing else that I do as a pastor is more important than leading God's people into His presence through praise and worship. God's people were created to experience and enjoy His presence. When people personally experience the majesty of God's presence, their lives are forever changed. It is through worship that we come into God's manifest presence therefore worship changes peoples lives.

A few moments in God's glory can bring more transformation into a life than years of "presenceless" church ministry. It is incumbent on the church not only to facilitate that worship but to make it their utmost priority, not an unimportant preliminary. God longs for intimacy with His people through praise and worship. Every successful encounter people have with God in worship produces an irreplaceable experience that results in eternal transformation.

Worshipping Churches Have a Worshipping Pastor

If worship is important in the life of a pastor, it will be important in the life of his or her church. If pastors worship, their churches will also worship. There is an unmistakable personal quality of character in the life of pastors who regularly and passionately worship. Brokenness, humility, holiness and compassion are the earmarks of a worshipping life. They will be present in the life of a pastor, if that pastor is a worshipper.

In much of the church we have a lopsided approach concerning ministry philosophy. The church tends to lean far too much on the human side of ministry presentation. Yes, we should work to create a comfortable and conducive atmosphere for people to worship in. But if, in the endeavor to make people feel comfortable, we create a more secular than sacred atmosphere where God's presence is unfelt, have we really succeeded?

I talk to pastors all the time who are desiring more of God's presence in their lives and churches. If a pastor has a hunger and a passion for more of God's presence, it will become a part of the attitude of the church also. If pastors become preoccupied with the "stuff" and business of ministry, they tend to grow less sensitive and even indifferent towards worship. I believe, in order to survive and succeed in ministry, every pastor must be a devoted and passionate worshipper in their private and public lives.

Ministry must not descend into the lesser realms of vocation and occupation. Instead it must remain the grand calling and supernatural experience of men and women who are being and bringing change by the presence of God through worshipping lifestyles.

Why Should the World Have All the Great Musicians?

But now bring me a musician. (2 Kings 3:15a)

I pioneered a church in Scottsdale, Arizona, in the eighties. God helped us as the church began to grow but I had a problem. I was very unhappy with the musical quality of the worship leader. (The inside joke is that I was the worship leader.)

After one Sunday morning service, I sat in a chair at my house and started to complain (I mean, pray) to God about it. I said something to Him like, "Lord, how come all the good musicians and singers are working in bars and nightclubs and not in churches? It seems like we're always decades behind in the church."

What happened next startled me and forever transformed my ministry. As clear as a bell, the Lord spoke to me and said, "Why don't you pray for unsaved and backslidden musicians to be saved and bring their talents into the church?"

In the next breath I did what the Lord had spoken to me. I began to pray for musicians to come into the church from the world. While I was praying, my phone began to ring. I got up to answer it and was shocked by who was on the other line. It was my old best friend from childhood. He and I were both P.K.'s (preacher' kids), and he became a very talented professional musician in Hollywood, California. We hadn't talked to or seen each other in more than ten years as our lives took vastly different paths. I told him what I had just been doing, praying for secular musicians to come to Christ and to the church. He and I both realized we were in a God-moment of time.

I continued to pray this very specific prayer for gifted musicians and singers to come into the Kingdom of God. Within a few months, something truly marvel u happened in our church. The owners of the biggest jazz night club in the Phoenix area were wondrously saved and became members of our church. Within a matter of weeks, the very best musicians in the Phoenix metropolitan area were playing and singing on our church platform. The rock-and-roll newspaper New Times did several very favorable articles on what had happened. The title of one front-page article said, "You'll Never Believe Where the Best Music in Phoenix Is."

Several of the members of that very special group are now well-known worship leaders across America (Israel Houghton, Ricardo Sanchez, George Chadwick and B.]. Putnam.) Since that time our church has never lacked for talented, skilled and anointed worship leaders and musicians. If your church needs help in its worship ministry, try praying the prayer that worked for us.

The Seven Levels of Praise

There are seven Hebrew words for "praise" in the Bible. These words represent different levels of praise as described below. Together they reveal a process to and perfection of our praise to our God. We are a "holy priesthood to offer up spiritual sacrifices acceptable to God through Jesus Christ." We have been anointed to be priests before God in order to bring the offering of our praises.

Level 1) Towdah: The Sacrifice of Thanksgiving

In Hebrew, towdah means "a sacrifice of thanksgiving that is demonstrated with an extension of the hand in adoration." To engage in towdah is to praise God whether you feel like it or not. It is a decision that leads to the action of praise. Notice how important praise is in the scripture:

Fundamental Doctrines	Number of Time Mentioned	Methods of Praise	Number of Time Mentioned
Virgin Birth	2	Dancing	5
Missions	12	Shouting	65
Justification	70	Thanksgiving	135
Sanctification	72	Singing	287
Baptism	80	Rejoicing	288
Repentance	110	Playing Instruments	317
2nd Coming of Christ	318	Praise	340

This comparison shows us that praise is important to God and absolutely necessary to His people. We are simply to be praising people.

> *Whoever offers praise glorifies Me; And to him who orders his conduct aright I will show the salvation of God. (Ps. 50:23)*

> *He who sacrifices thank offering honors me and he prepares the way sho that I many shew him the salvation of God.* (Ps. 50:23, NIV)

> *It is the praising life that honors Me. As soon as you set your foot on the way, I'll show you my salvation.* (Ps. 50:23, The MESSAGE)

Towdah praise is the lifting up of hands - palms cupped upward. It is the submission and surrender of our lives in order to bring the sacrifice of our praise. *Therefore by Him let us continually offer the sacrifice of praise to God, that is, the fruit of our lips, giving thanks to His name.* (Heb. 13:15; Emphasis mine)

Level 2) Yadah: Strong Praise

The Hebrew word yadah means "the action of extending our hands in power as we confess, praise, sing and give thanks to the nature and work of God." In yadah praise we feel and respond to the presence of God with strength. Towdah praise is a sacrifice, but yadah praise is a response to the awesome presence of our God. *Praise the Lord! I will praise the Lord with my whole heart, In the assembly of the upright and in the congregation.* (Ps. 111: 1) Yadah praise is enthusiastic and strong!

> *You meet him who rejoices and does righteousness, Who remembers You in Your ways. You are indeed angry, for we have sinned-- In these ways we*

> *continue; And we need to be saved.* (Is. 64:5; Emphasis mine)

> *Draw near to God and He will draw near to you. Cleanse your hands, you sinners; and purify your hearts, you double-minded.* (James 4:8; Emphasis mine)

God meets our sacrifice of praise with the strength of His presence!

Level 3) Zamar. Instrumental Praise

The Hebrew word zamar means "to touch the strings or part of a musical instrument, i.e., to play upon it; to make music with instruments accompanied by singing."

> *Let them praise His name with the dance; let them sing praises to Him with the timbrel and harp.* (Ps. 149:3)

> *Praise Him with the sound of the trumpet;*
> *Praise Him with the lute and harp!*
> *Praise Him with the timbrel and dance;*
> *Praise Him with stringed instruments and flutes!*
> *Praise Him with loud cymbals;*
> *Praise Him with clashing cymbals!* (Ps. 150:3-5)

> *Blessed be the Lord my Rock,*
> *Who trains my hands for war,*
> *And my fingers for battle ...* (Ps. 144:1)

> *"But now bring me a musician." Then it happened, when the musician played, that the hand of the Lord came upon him.* (2 Kings 3:15)

Level 4) Halal: Celebration Praise (Crazy Praise)

The Hebrew word halal means "to celebrate to glorify, to boast, to be clamorous, foolish, to rave, to shine." Hallaluis means Halal to Yah: to celebrate, boast and shine about Yah. Halal praise includes the physical expression of dancing, shouting, kneeling and bowing. It is praise that engages and releases our human emotion in celebration to God.

> *So David and all the house of Israel brought up the ark of the Lord with shouting and with the sound of the trumpet.* (2 Sam. 6: 15)

> *"So David said to Michal, lit was before the Lord, who chose me instead of your father and all his house, to appoint me ruler over the people of the Lord, over Israel. Therefore I will play music before the Lord. And I will be even more undignified than this, and will be humble in my own sight.'"* (2 Samuel 6:21-22; Emphasis mine)

> *Let my soul live, and it shall praise You; and let Your judgments help me.* (Ps. 119: 175)

> My soul shall be satisfied as with marrow and fatness, and my mouth shall praise You with joyful lips. (Ps. 63:5)

> I will give You thanks in the great assembly; I will praise You among many people. (Ps. 35:18)

> Let them exalt Him also in the assembly of the people, and praise Him in the company of the elders. (Ps. 107:32)

Level 5) Barak: Adoration Praise
The Hebrew word barak means "to kneel, to bless ad as an act of adoration." As we joyfully ascend the Hill of Zion. in our praise of God, we will reach the place of barak where our hearts are overcome with the goodness and glory of our God and the praise of adoration pours from our heart and lips. However many times the praise and place of barak is found in wordless worship.

Level 6) Tehillah: Spiritual Songs
Tehillah praise is "spiritual, spontaneous, songs of the spirit flowing in the presence of God." I asked the Lord what our praise was like to Him. He said "Most of my children's praise to me is like a Hallmark card: polite, well intended, thoughtful, but lacking the sincerity and intimacy that I long for from my people. I love to hear you praise me in your own words, not always in someone else's."

> But You are holy, enthroned in the praises (tehillah) of Israel. (Ps. 22:3; addition mine)

..the voice of joy and the voice of gladness, the voice of the bridegroom (Jesus) and the voice of the bride (the church)... (Jer. 33:11; Addition mine)

Tehillah praise is the personal, intimate dialogue between Jesus and His bride singing to each other. *And do not be drunk with wine, in which is dissipation; but be filled with the Spirit, speaking to one another in psalms and hymns and spiritual songs, singing and making melody in your heart to the Lord.* (Eph. 5: 18-19) Be filled with the spirit speaking to one another in:

1. Psalms
2. Hymns
3. Spiritual songs (tehillah)

Worshiping God in our heavenly languages is tehillah praise. *I will bless the Lord at all times; His praise shall continually be in my mouth.* (Ps. 34:1)

Level 7) Sabach: Shouting Praise

Sabach praise is the eruption of shouts of praise to God. *Oh, clap your hands, all you peoples! Shout to God with the voice of triumph! God has gone up with a shout, the Lord with the sound of a trumpet. Sing praises to God, sing praises! Sing praises to our King, sing praises!* (Ps. 47:1,5-6)

Sabach is much more than an emotional experience that leads to the release of physical shouts. Sabach is the reward of pursuing God through the other levels of praise. In sabach praise, God empowers us with heavenly authority to proclaim His will and kingdom on earth among men!

> *Let the saints be joyful in glory; let them sing aloud on their beds. Let the high praises of God be in their mouth, and a two-edged sword in their hand, to execute vengeance on the nations, and punishments on the peoples; to bind their kings with chains, and their nobles with fetters of iron; to execute on them the written judgment- this honor have all His saints. Praise the Lord!* (Ps. 149:5-9)

On the seventh day Joshua led Israel in a shout that brought the walls of Jericho down!

Level 7) Sabach - shouting praise. It is the reward of climbing all the other levels. In sabach praise, God empowers us with heavenly authority.

Level 6) Tehillah - spiritual songs. Spontaneous songs of the spirit; personal, intimate dialogue with God.

Level 5) Barak - adoration praise. Loving, sometimes wordless, expression of worship.

Level 4) Halal- celebration praise. Dancing, shouting, kneeling, bowing; praise with emotion.

Level 3) Zamar - instrumental praise. Praise with musical instruments.

Level 2) Yadah - strong praise. Feeling and responding to the presence of God.

Level 1) Towdah - the sacrifice of thanksgiving. A decision that leads to the action of praise whether we feel like it or not.

Worship Evangelism

One night almost 30 years ago I had gathered together a group of young people in my father's church for a night of worship. Seven or eight of us began to worship and continued to worship for several hours. No one else knew we were there. The outside lights were off, and we had parked our cars out of sight in the rear of the church. Late that night someone began to literally bang on the closed front doors of the church.

    As I opened the door, a man stood there and then asked if we could please help him. He said he was a backslidden minister who just happened to be driving by the church when, he said, something literally compelled him to turn into the empty parking lot and knock on the unlit door. He said that, after many years away from Christ, he was suddenly, desperately convicted of his need to repent and return to God. He was unable to drive a foot farther or live a moment longer without making things right with God. Some great force (the Holy Spirit) had powerfully apprehended him as he drove near the church.

    That night I learned a great lesson about the power of worship to change the atmosphere of people and places. That man was gloriously restored to Christ because of the atmosphere that a group of young people had created through worship. Worship opens the heavens in the places were we worship and opens the hearts of the people who worship. When anyone that doesn't know Jesus comes into an environment where He is being truly worshipped, they will encounter God's love and presence drawing them to receive salvation.

Healing Worship

God is omnipresent. He is everywhere at once. No matter where we go in this world, God's presence is there already. Although God's presence is everywhere, He only makes it known, visible and tangible when He is worshipped. This revelation of God always has in it His power to heal and to deliver. Where His presence is made known, healing will follow and lives will be made whole.

Worship heals. When hurting people come into the midst of a worshipping church, God's power and grace can touch their lives. Worship creates the environment for healing and for the flowing of the gifts of the Holy Spirit. To lead people into worship and then not give them an opportunity for the gifts of God's heavenly grace to flow, robs them of the life and wholeness God longs to give them. However we can properly, timely and orderly orchestrate worship for God's people, we must.

DR. MICHAEL MAIDEN

Dr. Michael Maiden and Mary, his beloved wife of 30 years, are the senior pastors of Church for the Nations in Phoenix, Arizona. Here he strongly and lovingly prepares God's people for service in God's Kingdom. The messages are always relevant, timely and life-changing as well as prophetic.

Dr. Maiden has earned both a Masters and Doctorate Degree in Christian Psychology. He has authored seven books including: The Joshua Generation: God's Manifesto for the End Time Church, and his most recent book, Turn the World Upside Down, which speaks to this present generation about the next step to be taken.

In addition to his work in the local church, he is a strong prophetic voice to this generation and has ministered to those holding Public Offices as well as Pastors and Ministers throughout the world. Dr. Maiden is President and CEO of Church On The Rock International – a dynamic ministry that oversees more than 6,000 churches worldwide. He is also on the board of Fishers of Men International, the Jewish Voice International and several local churches.

Made in the USA
San Bernardino, CA
19 August 2018